KANT'S THEORETICAL PHILOSOPHY

A COMMENTARY TO THE CENTRAL PART OF
THE 'CRITIQUE OF PURE REASON'

BY FELIX GRAYEFF

TRANSLATED FROM THE GERMAN BY
DAVID WALFORD

MANCHESTER
UNIVERSITY PRESS

BARNES & NOBLE INC
NEW YORK

Deutung und Darstellung der theoretischen Philosophie Kants
first published in West Germany, 1951, by
Felix Meiner Verlag, Hamburg

This translation copyright © 1970 MANCHESTER UNIVERSITY PRESS

Published by the University of Manchester at
THE UNIVERSITY PRESS
316–324 Oxford Road, Manchester M13 9NR

UK standard book number: 7190 0406 3 *(cloth binding)*
7190 0441 1 *(paperback)*

U.S.A.
BARNES & NOBLE INC
105 Fifth Avenue, New York, N.Y. 10003
US standard book number: 389 03988 8

Printed in Great Britain by
Butler & Tanner Ltd, Frome and London

CONTENTS

	Page
TRANSLATOR'S PREFACE	ix
FOREWORD	xi

INTRODUCTION

I Doubt about the unity of Kant's philosophy	1
II Logical unity as an object of interpretation	4
III The basic hypothesis of the explanation offered here	8
IV The *Critique of Pure Reason*: the whole and its parts	8

THE COMMENTARY

KANT'S INTRODUCTION
Section I	13
Section II	16
Section III	17
Section IV	19
Kant's reform of logic I	20
Section IV (continued)	22
Section V	24
Section VI	30
Section VII	33

TRANSCENDENTAL AESTHETIC
§ 1	37
§ 2	39
§ 3	43
Basic aspects of Kant's theory of time	46
§ 4	47
§ 5	50
§ 6	53
§ 7	55
§ 8	58

CONTENTS

§ 8 I	59
A comparison of Kant's philosophy with certain Greek views, and in particular with Aristotle's Metaphysics	64
§ 8 II	67
§ 8 III	68
§ 8 IV	71
Conclusion of the 'Transcendental Aesthetic'	73
The relation of the 'Transcendental Aesthetic' to the 'Transcendental Analytic'	74

TRANSCENDENTAL LOGIC

Metaphysical Deduction of the Categories	76
Introductory	76
I Logic in general	77
II Transcendental logic	81
III The division of general logic into analytic and dialectic	86
IV The division of transcendental logic into transcendental analytic and dialectic	88
Transcendental analytic	88
Analytic of concepts	88
The clue to the discovery of all pure concepts of the understanding	88
The logical employment of the understanding	90
Kant's reform of logic II	90
The logical employment of the understanding (continued)	95
§ 9	99
§ 10	105
§§ 11 and 12	116
§ 11	116
§ 12	118

KANT'S TRANSITION TO THE 'TRANSCENDENTAL DEDUCTION OF THE CATEGORIES'

§§ 13 and 14	120
§ 13	121
§ 14	124

TRANSCENDENTAL DEDUCTION OF THE CATEGORIES

Introductory	131
§ 15	134

CONTENTS

§ 16	138
§ 17	151
§ 18	155
§ 19	160
§ 20	166
§§ 21–27	169
§ 21	170
§§ 22 and 23	172
§ 22	172
§ 23	173
§ 24 I	176
§ 24 II	180
Kant's doctrine of the inner sense and the Self as appearance	184
§ 25	185
§ 26	187
Kant's theory of inherence and substance	195
Kant's theory of causality	196
§ 26 (continued)	200
§ 27	201
Kant's synopsis of the 'Transcendental Deduction'	204

PHENOMENA AND NOUMENA
Kant's unified theory of the thing-in-itself   205

SYNOPSIS OF KANT'S THEORETICAL PHILOSOPHY   215

INDEX   226

TRANSLATOR'S PREFACE

For the purposes of this translation Dr Grayeff has introduced a number of minor revisions to the original German edition. Two paragraphs have been added and one omitted. Dr Grayeff has also agreed to my enlarging the index. It is hoped that this will enhance the usefulness of the book.

In all direct quotations from Kant's *Critique of Pure Reason* I have used N. Kemp Smith's translation. Where Dr Grayeff proposes a revision to the text of the *Critique* I have indicated how the proposed revision would affect the Kemp Smith translation. All other quotations from Kant are my own translation. I have also followed Kemp Smith's translation of Kant's key terms where they occur in the body of the commentary itself, in order to avoid confusion.

In his commentary Dr Grayeff refers to particular passages of Kant's *Critique of Pure Reason* by numbering the paragraphs of sections and, not infrequently, the sentences within a paragraph. Although this numbering applies to the original German text, I have retained it. However, since it is unlikely that those using this English translation of Dr Grayeff's commentary will refer to Kant's original German text, I have indicated in square brackets the corresponding paragraphs and sentences in the Kemp Smith translation where there is a divergence between the two.

Finally, I should like to express my thanks to Dr Grayeff for the great care with which he has corrected this translation and suggested improvements to it.

D. E. WALFORD

FOREWORD

This book has two purposes: its first intention is to present an account of Kant's theoretical philosophy as a logically consistent whole. The second intention is to develop a method of interpretation which contains within it the laws of system-building thought, thereby revealing these laws as the very principles of logical unity in general.

FELIX GRAYEFF

To my wife

To my wife

INTRODUCTION

I *Doubt about the unity of Kant's philosophy*

There has been some dispute as to whether Kant's theoretical philosophy can be understood as a consistent whole. Kant's disciples and immediate successors developed the views of philosophical Idealism. On the other hand, August Comte, the founder of Positivism, maintained that it was he who was the true successor of the critical school of thought. What could be a more natural suspicion than to suppose that the *Critique of Pure Reason* itself contained the antithesis between Idealism and Realism? This suspicion seemed all the more likely since it was apparently confirmed by Hegel's dialectic (even its most bitter opponents were unable to free themselves from its influence). Philosophical progress seemed conceivable only in terms of the negation of existing views. But no one had radically disputed Kant's teaching or rejected it as a whole. One could only conclude that the indispensable antithesis was to be found within Kant's system itself. Kant had repeatedly maintained that his work was an altogether consistent whole and that apparent contradictions were the exclusive product of misunderstanding or precipitate judgement.[1] None the less, even in Kant's own lifetime, doubts about the thorough consistency of his system were repeatedly voiced. This was not forgotten later.

It would appear that Schopenhauer was the first to give a definite form to these doubts. He claimed to be able to

---

[1] See Kant's preface to his *Metaphysische Anfangsgründe der Naturwissenschaft*; see Kant's preface to the second edition of the *Critique of Pure Reason*, where Kant also expressly emphasises that none of the alterations made by him have any bearing on his meaning; they only affect the exposition (B XXXVII ff.).

specify two divergent lines of thought in Kant's text itself. He compared the two editions of the *Critique of Pure Reason*. He extolled the pure idealistic philosophy of the first edition but denounced the second edition (particularly the chapter 'Phenomena and Noumena') as a betrayal by the ageing Kant of his own deeper insights.[2]

Schopenhauer's view that Kant never finally decided between Idealism and Realism was adopted by Kuno Fischer. Since then it has dominated Kantian scholarship. This view has led to the almost unshakable conviction that Kant's thought embodies a fundamental contradiction. Indeed, it turned out to be the starting point of an analytical criticism which seems to have run wild.[3] Nor was it only

---

[2] Cf. commentary to the chapter 'Phenomena and Noumena'. Cf. also the footnote to p. 133.

[3] Kant, in a letter to Moses Mendelssohn, 18 August 1783, relates how he wrote the *Critique of Pure Reason* in four or five months. This letter is frequently cited as proof against the unity of Kant's work. Kant scholars have argued that no one could possibly have composed a work as long and profound as the *Critique of Pure Reason* in such a short time. It is hence, they argue, futile to look for a consistent theory in Kant; the *Critique of Pure Reason* is simply a collection of earlier articles and notes; it is full of obscurities and deep-rooted, irresolvable contradictions.

Now it is certainly true that parts of the *Critique of Pure Reason*, including the whole of the second half of the work, the 'Transcendental Dialectic', were composed before 1780. However, the crucial first half, the 'Introduction', the German version of the 'Transcendental Aesthetic', the 'Transcendental Analytic', with the 'Metaphysical' and 'Transcendental Deductions', perhaps even the chapter of the 'Schematism' and the 'Analogies' (A 1 to A 130; A 148 to A 226) must have been written in one effort during those four or five months—unless Kant's own assertion is to be dismissed as completely misleading. These parts contain Kant's most important ideas and proofs. The rest is scarcely more than amplification and application.

There seems to be no difficulty in assuming that, already before 1780, Kant had a sufficiently clear idea of his own philosophy as a whole to write the second half of the *Critique of Pure Reason* before he was able to write the first. The second part is less concise, more didactic and even, on occasion, rhetorical. By contrast, the style of the first half reveals an impatient brevity, along with the utmost precision and an extreme accuracy of expression. The section A 1 to A 130 cannot fail to strike a

INTRODUCTION

Realism and Idealism which were found unreconciled in Kant's *magnum opus*. Other unresolved antitheses were also discovered: between Empiricism and Rationalism (Hume and Leibniz); between a metaphysics based on mathematical principles and one based on logical principles (Newton and Leibniz). Contradictions were found between the two main divisions of the first part of the *Critique of Pure Reason* —indeed, contradictions were detected within almost every important section. Kant was accused of presenting his reader with two different philosophies: one in the 'Transcendental Aesthetic' and the other in the 'Transcendental Analytic'. Kant was accused of arguing in one enormous vicious-circle fallacy in maintaining that the understanding determines nature and nature the understanding (cf. p. 120 ff., especially p. 126 f.). Scholars claimed to be able to detect the different stages of Kant's philosophical development in the text of the *Critique of Pure Reason* (particularly in the first edition of the 'Transcendental Deduction'). It was asserted that Kant's work was a 'patchwork' of notes, collected over a period of twelve years, summarily thrown together and never unified into a consistent whole.[4]

---

sensitive reader as one piece, written in a single period of high enthusiasm. One can only conclude from the above-mentioned letter that Kant originally wrote A 1 to A 130—and perhaps A 148 to A 226 too— during those four or five months. During those same months he also arranged the rest, and by inserting connective sentences and sections welded the whole into a single book. This he did in accordance with a plan which had been slowly maturing over a period of eleven years.

[4] This theory was first proposed by Adickes and Vaihinger. It was developed to its extreme limits and apparently proved in detail by N. Kemp Smith in his celebrated *A Commentary to Kant's Critique of Pure Reason* (London, 1918). By contrast, it is the great merit of H. J. Paton in his *Kant's Metaphysic of Experience* (London, 1936), to have postulated the unity of the *Critique of Pure Reason* and to have defended, with deep conviction, Kant's reputation in England. I am happy to admit that one of the crucial stimuli to the writing of the present book was Paton's commentary, in particular his emphasis on the necessity of an exact running commentary to the *Critique of Pure Reason*. The reader will find mention of these two books in the course of the following commentary.

The aim of this commentary is to prove the complete—i.e. fully achieved—unity of the *Critique of Pure Reason*. All suggestion of compromise is rejected. The intention is to show that every sentence of the *Critique of Pure Reason* is consistent both with itself and with every other sentence in the book, and that the critical theory as a whole harmonises with all its parts; in other words, that it is possible to give a comprehensive account of Kant's theoretical philosophy and that every sentence and every argument of the *Critique of Pure Reason* can be satisfactorily fitted into this account.

The following commentary implicitly rejects the view that unity is something which can never be reached, that it is something transcendent; that since thought is in continual flux, unity must always remain something to which we aspire—an unattainable ideal of reconciling the finite and the infinite. This book, on the contrary, is based on the concept of immanent formal unity, the unity of a successfully completed work of thought. Only by assuming such unity is it at all possible to re-think and re-prove an already completed system of thought; only on this assumption is it possible to set out anew from its starting point and to arrive once more at its ultimate conclusion—*its* conclusion and no other.

II *Logical unity as an object of interpretation*

Interpretation, as a means of research into works of literature and philosophy, is, in general terms, an attempt to re-create a unique product of the human mind. The purpose of such interpretation is to open the way to an understanding of the work in question. Such a re-creation is generally achieved by making the ideas implicit in the work explicit; more precisely, by clarifying the explicit ideas of the work through its implicit ideas. Various kinds of interpretation may, however, be distinguished or developed, depending on the presuppositions of the interpretation or on the kind of knowledge at which the interpretation aims. It is thus possible to look at a work from a

INTRODUCTION

historical point of view, or it can be examined from the standpoint of the writer's development: one may try to discover the historical circumstances and connections within the work, or to grasp the creative vision of the thinker or artist, as it is variously expressed in the work.

This kind of interpretation has been rightly described as an infinite task. It has shown itself peculiarly unsuitable to the task of clarifying the *Critique of Pure Reason*. Far from producing a slowly deepening appreciation of the coherence of Kant's theory, it has strengthened the view that Kant's work is self-contradictory. Indeed, it has led to the opinion that Kant was utterly and totally confused.

Let us assume that we wish to discover the unity of a philosophical work. It is not enough for us to look at the work in question as a product of various historical circumstances, nor as a product of the author's intellectual development (nor even as a mixture of truth and falsity). We must look at it as an attempt on the author's part to give a consistent and coherent answer to certain basic questions: we must look at it as a logical unity. We must accordingly try to construct a method of interpreting the work with that end in view.

Logical unity consists in the harmony of an ultimately inferred concept with certain basic elementary concepts through the mediation of intermediate concepts. One might also say that logical unity is the harmony of an ultimate proposition with certain basic elementary propositions through the mediation of intermediate propositions. Thus, if we want to grasp the logical unity of a work or if we presuppose the logical unity of that work, we must assume that it will be possible (1) to describe the final conclusion as an all-embracing central concept and (2) to describe certain concepts as mediating concepts.

The interpretation of a work consists in describing its explicit concepts or propositions from the implicit viewpoint of the author. Thus, to reproduce the logical unity of a work, or to re-think a coherent and consistent system of thought, it is necessary (1) to understand the explicit concepts (elementary and intermediate) as reflecting a unifying concept, namely, the ultimate conclusion; in other words, *we must construe the ultimate conclusion as a concept universally implicit throughout the work*. We must also (2) describe the explicit (or elementary) concepts from the viewpoint of certain mediating concepts; we must show that these mediating concepts are both contained in all the basic elementary concepts and that they also contain within themselves the ultimate conclusion.

In this way, the interpretation acquires a logically constructive character. Instead of looking for the (infinite number of) concepts which may be contained in the ultimate conclusion—instead, that is, of analysing a philosophical work step by step in order to reconstruct it step by step—we shall attempt to find the ultimate conclusion in the elementary and intermediate concepts, and thus to reconstruct the philosophical work without having first analysed it. Or, to put it differently: we shall reconstruct a philosophical work by starting simultaneously from its answer (the ultimate conclusion and the intermediate concepts) and its questions (the basic elementary concepts).[5]

I shall apply this principle of interpretation to the *Critique of Pure Reason*. In doing so I intend to regard the final critical conclusion, the proposition or concept of the synthetic unity of apperception,[6] as the single implicit concept which is to be discovered and made explicit in all parts of the *Critique of Pure Reason*. Furthermore, I shall be looking only for the concept which mediates between the elementary (to be determined) concept and the ultimate conclusion. In this way, the interpretation ceases to be an infinite task. Its aim is finite: it wishes to discover only *one* universally

---

[5] Cf. the 'question-and-answer logic' which R. G. Collingwood developed for his own use, as he recounts in his *Autobiography*, pp. 29 ff. (Oxford, 1939).

[6] See §§ 16 and 17.

implicit concept and a finite number of intermediate concepts. This means that my interpretation does not aim to discover all the concepts which are contained, actually or potentially, in Kant's philosophy. Its only aim is to reveal the logical structure of the critical philosophy as intended and realised by Kant.

In this way, my interpretation does not aim at logic in the traditional sense; it does not even aim at the logic taught by Kant. It aims at the logic suggested by an examination of the *Critique of Pure Reason*. In other words, this enquiry is based on no other assumption and has no other object than the concept of logic itself, the concept of coherent thought in general.

I wish to maintain that an intellectual system can only be re-thought by making the ultimate conclusion everywhere explicit by means of the intermediate concepts. It is not possible within the limits of this book to show that this principle of interpretation can also be so formulated that it is applicable to original coherent thought in general.[7]

I can now finally say how I intend to prove the unity of the *Critique of Pure Reason*:

1. I shall show that each doctrinal[8] proposition of the book can be transformed into an 'interpretational' definition, either of the type SP=M *sub notione* C (central concept),[9] or of the type SP=MC *sub notione* C′,[10] or of the type SP not=MC, MC′.[11]

2. I shall show (*a*) that all PM, irrespective of content, can be described as intuition or, more precisely, as a (successive) multiplicity of representations referring to

[7] This I have tried to prove in my *Versuch über das Denken*, Hamburg, 1966.
[8] In contrast to the digressions and the didactic and rhetorical explanations.
[9] Where S is experience, knowledge; space, time; a (pure) concept of the understanding.
[10] Where S is a theoretical concept of reason.
[11] Where S is the thing-in-itself.

three-dimensional externality; (b) that C is always the synthetic unity of apperception, and C' unity is a concept of reason.[12]

Unless we look for unity we shall not find it. Only by adopting the unity of the *Critique of Pure Reason* as our hypothesis can we hope to prove it. It is thus the object of this commentary to reveal the teaching of Kant, not as content, but as form; not as a mixture of truth and falsity, to be either confirmed or refuted as the case may be, but as a system of ideas to be understood and reconstructed; not as the uncertain product of Kant's incompleted reflections, but as Kant's living thought, directed towards a *single* goal and expressed in definitive form.

III *The basic hypothesis of the explanation offered here*

The basic hypothesis of the present interpretation of the *Critique of Pure Reason* may be formulated as follows. Space and time are media indeterminately given but categorically determined by a synthetic act of the understanding; their determination takes the form of duration, simultaneity and ordered succession, of spatial unity, divisible and measurable. These categorical determinations, in their turn, determine the matter given to the senses.

IV *The* Critique of Pure Reason: *the whole and its parts*

Kant's philosophy may be regarded as an original solution to the basic problem of all Western philosophy: the problem of the relation of thought and reality. Kant's answer, to put it briefly, consists in the theory that thought generates phenomenal reality by means of space and time; true Being, however, must remain for ever unknown to us.

Kant's philosophy may also be described as a reinterpre-

---

[12] I do not of course mean that I shall actually transform Kant's text into definitions of this kind. Such a procedure would make the commentary unreadable. What I mean is that Kant's text *can* be transformed into definitions of the kind in question—and it is this that the commentary is intended to prove.

INTRODUCTION

tation of the ancient classical concepts of form and matter. Kant, while freeing the thing-in-itself from the determinations of form and matter, maintains that phenomenal reality is a compound of form (thought) and matter (sensations spatially and temporally bound). Neither pure form nor pure matter can ever be objects of human knowledge. Hence, for us, form is always form forming matter, and matter matter formed. Thus, according to Kant, the basic difference between thought and reality is the difference between thought as form forming matter and phenomenal reality as matter formed.

But, according to Kant, there is a third element to be taken into account: intuition (or space and time). Intuition stands between pure thought and pure matter. Its mediation makes possible both the transformation of matter into phenomenal reality in accordance with certain immutable laws, and the manifestation of pure thought as the form of the knowable categories. The theory that space and time are universal media, i.e. elements serving as matter to thought and determining sensuous matter as form, is one of Kant's most striking contributions to philosophy. It is also the pivotal point of Kant's whole system.

Kant did not think that he had creatively constructed his philosophy; his view was that he had discovered it by a process of methodical analysis. He accordingly presents his theory in the following way: he starts from organised nature as it is experienced and goes on to discover the formal or determining elements inherent in organised nature. In the 'Transcendental Aesthetic' Kant discovers (determinate) space and time: they are the elements which form nature. In the 'Metaphysical Deduction of the Categories' he discovers the logical forms inherent in judgement—the categories: they are the determinants which form space and time. In the 'Transcendental Deduction of the Categories' he shows that unified representation or determinate consciousness is nothing other than the intuitional forms of space and time, determined in accordance with the categories;

KANT'S THEORETICAL PHILOSOPHY

and consequently that the human mind, by determining itself categorically, generates the picture of organised nature harmonising with immutable laws.

Every part of the *Critique of Pure Reason* reflects, each from its own peculiar standpoint, Kant's basic distinction between that which forms and that which is formed.

In the 'Introduction', knowledge of nature is discussed both as experience of organised nature and as certainty of the principles organising nature. In the 'Transcendental Aesthetic' space and time are treated both as organised (determinate) magnitudes and as organising (determining) media. In the 'Transcendental Analytic', the mind is discussed both as receptivity corresponding to organised nature and as spontaneity referring to the organising form (concept). In the 'Metaphysical Deduction of the Categories' logic is treated both as general logic concerned with already formed concepts and as transcendental logic whose object is the formative concept (the category). In the 'Transcendental Deduction of the Categories', where Kant gives the final account of his theory and attempts to establish its truth, consciousness is treated both as organised consciousness identical with organised nature and as our spontaneously organising and validly constructing faculty, the highest organ of apperception. Kant also discusses objective nature both as necessarily connected and as spontaneously formed by the act of synthesis. Finally, in the 'Transcendental Dialectic' Kant discusses the theoretical concept in general, both as a concept of the understanding equivalent to synthetic unity first realising itself in the infinite and as a concept of reason which is the postulated finite unity.

One final remark: the synopsis of Kant's argument at the end of the book is intended to serve two purposes: (1) to facilitate an understanding of my interpretation of the text and (2) to present the general argument of Kant's theoretical philosophy as a unity.

THE COMMENTARY

KANT'S INTRODUCTION

SECTION I

Introductory

Kant here explains the critical significance of the terms '*a priori*', '*a posteriori*' and 'pure and mixed knowledge *a priori*'. The distinction which Kant makes here between *a priori* and *a posteriori* is the basic critical distinction between thought and phenomenal reality, between form forming matter and matter formed, between organising spontaneity (of thought) and organised nature.

Résumé

While it is, of course, true that one can describe nature as simply nature experienced, it is not *our* intention to represent nature experienced as the uniform and original source of all our knowledge. On the contrary, our purpose is to look at nature as we experience it from two points of view: (1) as organised nature and (2) as organisation or (logical) form, which we impose on nature through the two media of intuition, space and time. It is in connection with this basic distinction that the terms '*a priori*' and '*a posteriori*' are introduced. Knowledge relating to organisation and (logical) form forming matter is called *a priori* knowledge. Knowledge relating to organised nature (matter formed) is called *a posteriori* knowledge. We also distinguish between pure and mixed knowledge *a priori*. Pure knowledge *a priori* is knowledge of thought manifested in the pure media. Mixed knowledge *a priori* is knowledge of thought manifested in the materially filled media, i.e. in the phenomenal world.

Explanation

FIRST AND SECOND PARAGRAPHS It is, of course, true, Kant begins, that all our knowledge is permeated with experience of organised nature—indeed, psychologically speaking, experience precedes all possible knowledge. None the less, we can still ask whether we cannot perhaps find elements which, although contained in experience, yet also construct and form it. In other words, although we must, of course, start from organised nature (matter formed) we can still try to distinguish organisation (form forming matter) from organised nature.

One question forces itself upon us from the beginning. Why did not Kant, for expository purposes, sharply distinguish matter as the indeterminate element and organising form, i.e. category or thought? In making this distinction he could have treated the media of intuition, space and time, from both points of view. If Kant had chosen to make his basic distinction in this way his work would certainly have been more easily intelligible. The reason why he presented his philosophy in the way he did lies deep. Kant had to present his philosophy as if he were discovering and proving it. If he had chosen the method outlined above it would inevitably have looked as if he were constructing his philosophy. By starting from organised nature as it is experienced, Kant appears to be discovering the formal elements contained in nature. Had he started from indeterminate nature—i.e. from nature as pure matter and from formative thought (the category)—it would inevitably have looked as if his argument were based on arbitrary presuppositions; it would have looked as if he were constructing a picture or concept of nature which was neither necessary nor exclusively (objectively) valid.

THIRD PARAGRAPH Kant now introduces the two basic critical terms '*a priori*' and '*a posteriori*' (cf. résumé). If a basic distinction is made between spontaneity of thought and nature, organised or yet to be organised, and if space and time are treated as the 'primary matter' or media of intuition (cf. commentary to 'Transcendental Aesthetic', p. 37), then knowledge relating to thought manifested in space and time is *a priori* knowledge. Such knowledge is independent of experience, independent of the 'secondary matter' which fills space and time. *A posteriori* knowledge relates, not to nature as a spatio–temporal entity nor to nature as a set of spatio–temporal relations, but to nature in its fullness, i.e. the nature to which our senses react in so many different ways.

FOURTH PARAGRAPH Kant emphasises that he does not use the term '*a priori*' in its generally accepted traditional sense. In Kant's time the term '*a priori*' was traditionally used in two senses: a logical, and a metaphysical sense. In its logical sense the term referred to knowledge not derived from immediate observation but deduced, i.e. inferred, from other knowledge. Leibniz uses the term '*a priori*' in its metaphysical sense; he makes the original knowledge of substance an attribute of the divine Creator.

According to Kant, *a priori* knowledge is derived neither immediately nor indirectly from observation; nor is it an attribute of God. *A priori* knowledge, for Kant, refers to the spontaneous activity of the human understanding by means of which experience is formed. It is an attribute of man the creator.

Kant here compares his use of the term '*a priori*' with traditional logical usage only. (In connection with Kant's reinterpretation of the term '*a priori*' in its metaphysical sense, cf. the 'Synopsis', p. 215.)

FIFTH PARAGRAPH The full significance of the further distinction between pure and mixed knowledge *a priori* will become clear later. Pure knowledge *a priori* is mathematical knowledge. Geometrical knowledge, for example, is simply logic manifested in the pure medium of space (cf. 'Transcendental Aesthetic'). Mixed knowledge *a priori* is logic applied to nature (through space and time); it is logic manifested in the materially filled forms of intuition (cf. § 26). An example of mixed knowledge *a priori* is the category of causality applied to any event (i.e. change) which can occur in nature (cf. commentary to § 26).

SECTION II

Résumé

A priori knowledge has two mutually implicative characteristics: necessity and universal applicability. If organised nature is understood as nature organised by thought, then nature is construed as necessarily organised (by ineluctable law), and thought is regarded as universally applied.

A priori knowledge, actually accessible to us both in the form of *a priori* judgement and *a priori* concept, always corresponds to the categories manifested in space and time.

Explanation

The two characteristics of *a priori* knowledge discussed by Kant belong originally and exclusively to logic. In a system of philosophy which maintains that phenomenal reality is constructed by logic, the above properties of necessity and universality also belong to the principles underlying the construction, i.e. they belong to the original forms of thought manifested in the universal media and applied to matter.

Kant adds that universal validity is often easier to understand than necessity (or: limited validity is often easier to prove than the absence of necessity, i.e. contingency). For example, it will be more readily admitted that every change has a cause than that every change must have a cause.

In fact, the two characteristics are mutually implicative (cf. résumé). None the less, an eighteenth-century reader, familiar with the doctrines and methods of inductive empiricism and, in particular, with the ideas of Hume, and new to the philosophy and transcendental method of Kant,

KANT'S INTRODUCTION

would probably be more willing to admit the universal validity of the causal principle than to concede its inherent necessity.

In the second paragraph of this section Kant draws attention to the fact that we actually possess knowledge with the characteristics in question: (1) in the field of mathematics and (2) in the field of common knowledge. To illustrate the latter, Kant once more chooses the causal principle—a principle certainly possessing the two characteristics.

The rest of this second paragraph contains repeated references to certain important consequences of the critical philosophy. For example, the allusion to Hume hints at Kant's doctrines of time, substance and causality. Each of these doctrines is closely related to the corresponding theories of Hume. (On Kant's relation to Hume, cf. commentary to §§ 19 and 26.)

Finally, Kant's discussion of objects in general—as distinct from substances constructed of inherences in time—anticipates the important discussions in §§ 21–23, where he considers the possibility of the category manifesting itself in a sensible medium other than time (and space). The category manifested in sensible media in general is the object in general. The *a priori* concept is the category manifested in time and space. 'Body' (in the mathematical sense of the word), for example, is simply the category (of quantity) manifested in space and time; 'substance' is the pure category (of substance) manifested in time (cf. résumé).

SECTION III

Résumé

The ultimate task of philosophy is to guide the human mind with respect to the ideas of God, freedom and immortality.

But can it be said that the guidance so given is based on knowledge?

KANT'S THEORETICAL PHILOSOPHY

Since knowledge is to be construed as valid construction in accordance with the rules of logic, and since, therefore, the means to knowledge must be construed as constructive logic (synthetic judgement), our task is (1) to distinguish constructive from non-constructive logic; these two kinds of logic are easily confused and such confusion has frequently led to spurious metaphysical speculations; (2) to establish whether there can be knowledge independently of experience, i.e. whether there can be *a priori* knowledge based exclusively on constructive logic; (3) to discover the conditions limiting such *a priori* knowledge.

Explanation

In this section—which, apart from the two subsequently added introductory paragraphs, constitutes the first chapter of the first edition—Kant formulates his problem. He does so in a form which, given his historical position, expresses its great significance most clearly and strikingly. He asks, 'Is (traditional) metaphysics possible? Or which sort of metaphysics is possible, i.e. in what sense may we say that we possess metaphysical knowledge?'

In order to solve this problem Kant begins by remarking that basically the problem is one of logic; more precisely, of the nature and applicability of logic. In section IV Kant discusses the difference between the two kinds of logic, one of which leads to new knowledge while the other does not.

The ultimate task of all philosophy, Kant here asserts, is to clarify the concepts of God, freedom and immortality. (In connection with Kant's concept of God—the 'Ideal of Pure Reason'—cf. commentary to the chapter 'Phenomena and Noumena' and the 'Synopsis'.) According to Kant, we cannot achieve knowledge about God or the concepts of freedom and immortality (the postulates of practical reason) comparable with the knowledge we can achieve of physical phenomena. And yet these concepts are treated in traditional metaphysics as if we did possess knowledge about them. All knowledge is based on logic. Our first task is therefore to investigate logic as the foundation (or instrument) of all our knowledge. The purpose of the investigation is to establish (1) which kind of logic (form of thought; judgement) may be regarded as a means to knowledge, (2) whether knowledge, exclusively based on such (constructive) logic, is accessible to us, and (3) under what conditions knowledge is possible for us. Kant's philosophical achievement may be described in various ways. One could, for example, say that by placing logic and metaphysics in a new relationship he created a new logic and a new metaphysics. Kant himself, however, characterises his philosophy as an investigation into the foundation of our knowledge.

Accordingly, he later describes the result of his investigation as the determination of the limits of our knowledge. Although we really do possess *a priori* knowledge, i.e. although logic is independent of experience, such knowledge (i.e. thought) is useless outside the field of experience. Thought can only lead to knowledge in so far as it is applied to the realm of possible experience.

SECTION IV

Résumé

We distinguish analytic and synthetic judgements; we also differentiate between synthetic *a posteriori* and synthetic *a priori* judgements.

An analytic judgement refers to the formed concept, i.e.— insofar as it is a concept of the understanding—to the determinate (and filled) forms of intuition. It describes the formed concept as implying another concept, or as an identical concept definable as different concepts. A synthetic *a posteriori* judgement refers to an empirical concept; more precisely, to a concept to be formed by empirical synthesis.

Finally, the synthetic *a priori* judgement refers to the given (indeterminate) forms of intuition. It determines indeterminate space and time. A mixed judgement *a priori* universally describes material nature as determinate space and time.

Explanation

It is, of course, only within the framework of Kant's reform of logic that his famous distinction between analytic and synthetic judgements—as also his equally celebrated theory of synthetic *a priori* judgements—can be understood.

KANT'S REFORM OF LOGIC I[1]

We have described traditional logic as the logic of Being and Kant's logic as the logic of phenomenal reality or valid construction. That is to say, we are maintaining that thought was traditionally represented as imitating reality (Being) whereas Kant's logic regards thought as constructing phenomenal reality.

In the traditional logic of Being the concept (substance) is understood as an ultimate unity under which inherences are subsumed through judging. In Kant's logic the concept (substance) is regarded as a synthetic unity to be constructed from inherences. Hence, in traditional logic, diversity within the concept amounts to contradiction and self-negation; in Kant's logic such diversity is not only conceivable but actually unavoidable. Whereas traditional logic construes the concept as unity and sharply separates A from B, Kant's logic construes the concept as synthetic unity and not only permits the union of A and B but actually regards it as necessary.

None the less, Kant incorporates traditional logic into his own system in the following way. By reinterpreting the logic of Being (original unity) as a logic of constructed reality (unity resting on antecedent synthesis), Kant devises a logic with two modes of thought: (1) the constructive mode (validly constructive thought), and (2) the

[1] Continued on p. 90.

secondary and derivative mode (clarificatory and verificatory thought relating to already constructed phenomenal reality). The constructive mode is construed as transcendental logic, the clarificatory and verificatory mode as general logic.[2] Traditional (general) logic is given a quite specific function within Kantian logic. It serves both as a means of clarifying concepts resulting from antecedent acts of constructive thought and as a means of testing, i.e. confirming and refuting, judgements likewise arising from antecedent acts of constructive thought.

We have now arrived at the distinction between analytic and synthetic judgements.

An analytic judgement is merely a clarificatory judgement. It refers to an already formed concept, whether *a priori* or *a posteriori*. It is an abstracting judgement and is always derivative. (When Kant comes to explain the working of apperception through the category he shows that even *a priori* concepts, to which analytic judgements refer, are based on original acts of synthesis; cf. §§ 10 and 15.)

An *a posteriori* judgement is never analytic. It would be absurd to say that I could arrive at an empirical concept by mere analysis or clarification of thought. Nor is an empirical synthetic judgement ever constructive. It is reconstructive. It is based both on antecedent abstraction and on antecedent synthesis. It constructs an empirical concept by means of general concepts arising from abstracting judgements; the abstraction, however, is based on original construction or synthesis.

Let us suppose, for example, that on the basis of given sensations we have constructed (by an act of apprehension; cf. the commentary to § 26) the empirical synthetic representation of a house in accordance with the category of quantity. But we must still explain this representation. We

[2] Judgement in the constructive mode is never abstracting but always subsuming judgement, which is reinterpreted as synthetic judgement. Judgement in the secondary mode of thought embraces the two types of abstracting and subsuming judgements.

can do so, for example, by abstracting the (general) concept 'cube' from a number of empirical cubes, and by then subsuming our representation 'house' under the general concept 'cube'. This final subsuming judgement is to be regarded as a synthetic *a posteriori* judgement; by its means we extend or even first form our empirical concept (and subsequently our knowledge) of 'house'.

Both an empirical concept (the product of synthetic *a posteriori* judgements) and an *a priori* concept (the product of a synthesis originally carried out in time and space) can be objects of analytic judgements. In other words, traditional (general) logic can refer either to empirical or to *a priori* concepts.

Finally, a synthetic *a priori* judgement is essentially ultimate and non-derivative (even though some synthetic *a priori* judgements may be based on other synthetic *a priori* judgements, as is for example the case in geometry). A synthetic *a priori* judgement is neither a means of clarifying concepts nor a means of testing judgements. It is rather a means of forming concepts, of determinately constructing space and time. It is purely constructive in character.

It is with the concept of the synthetic *a priori* judgement that Kant is concerned. The great revolution for which he was responsible is made tangible by this concept. In it is expressed the theory of the valid construction of phenomenal reality. The act which produces a synthetic *a priori* judgement is, in fact, the transcendental act which organises space and time in accordance with the category; it is the act which gives nature its fundamental law (cf. commentary to the 'Transcendental Aesthetic', especially pp. 73 f., with note 14, and also the commentary to § 26).

SECTION IV (*continued*)

Explanation

FIRST PARAGRAPH In distinguishing between analytic and synthetic judgements, we are looking at the concept from

KANT'S INTRODUCTION

two points of view: (1) as an already formed concept, i.e. as a concept implying several equated concepts; (2) as a concept which has still to be formed, i.e. as several (different) concepts which have to be combined into a single concept. For example, the judgement 'bodies are extended' is to be construed as a judgement relating to the first kind of concept. The concept 'body' is simply that of determinate space; it is equivalent to the category manifested in time and space. Similarly, the concept of extension coincides with that of space.

On the other hand, the judgement 'bodies are heavy' is to be regarded as relating to the second kind of concept. The different concepts of 'determinate space' and 'weight' are combined together into a single concept (namely that of 'body always having weight') (cf. § 19).

SECOND PARAGRAPH The synthetic *a posteriori* judgement is a means of combining different concepts into one. The union of these different concepts, although accidental, is permanent. Such union or combination is based on experience, i.e. determinate nature. Within determinate nature, the phenomenon of bodies always having weight is a determinate phenomenon; one can say that the empirical concept of such a phenomenon is formed by a synthetic *a posteriori* judgement based on a great number of observations of heavy bodies. Kant's definitive explanation of the peculiarly logical character of this kind of judgement is to be found in § 19.

THIRD PARAGRAPH By contrast, synthetic *a priori* judgements are not based on experience (determinate nature). Kant chooses the judgement 'every event has a cause' as an example of a synthetic *a priori* judgement. Kant describes this judgement as the union of two different concepts: (1) the concept of an event in the phenomenal world, and (2) the concept of causality.

This may be explained as follows: Kant describes the concept of change in two ways: (1) as an event in the phenomenal world, and (2) as a logical principle. It is easy to see that this twofold description reflects Kant's basic distinction between matter formed (organised nature) and form (organising thought).

The concept of 'change in nature' is thus split into two different concepts, both of which are to be regarded as determinate. The question is, how is the union of the two concepts to be explained? In what sense can one assert that one of the two concepts, the *a priori* principle, determines the other, the event in the phenomenal world? In raising this question we are also asking: in what sense can the event in the phenomenal world (nature undergoing changes) be described as indeterminate and determinable? What is the medium, the unknown X—Kant himself raises the question in this form—upon which the understanding bases its synthesising judgement?

The medium, the unknown X, is time. For nature can be construed as time, i.e. as an indeterminate succession which has to be logically organised. But nature, regarded as logically organised time, i.e. as determinate succession, is nature continually changing in accordance with a principle—the principle of causality (cf. commentary to § 26).

SECTION V

Résumé

We construe all mathematical propositions, both arithmetical and geometrical, as synthetic *a priori* judgements. But we construe mathematical axioms, such as $a = a$ and $(a + b) > a$, as basic logical principles realised in space and time through acts of synthesis.

We describe arithmetical and geometrical propositions as equations of the determinate forms of intuition and representations of logically determined quantity; or as determinations of space by means of logically and quantitatively ordered time.

Axioms, on the other hand, are to be construed as the

logical principle of identity realised in space and time; i.e. axioms are nothing other than the representations of identity resulting from the transformation of the media into identical synthetic unities.

The principles of pure physics must also be described as synthetic *a priori* judgements. For example, the doctrine of the conservation of matter is simply the equation of materially filled space with synthetically determined time.

Finally, traditional metaphysics seems to rest on synthetic *a priori* judgements. (The object of the critical investigation is to show whether such judgements are in fact possible in the field of metaphysics.)

Explanation

Kant's assertion that mathematical propositions, both arithmetical and geometrical, are synthetic, has frequently been attacked. The most varied attempts have been made to refute this part of Kant's doctrine. I do not here intend to enter into a discussion of this problem either with Kant or his critics. I shall only attempt to show in what sense mathematical propositions may be construed as synthetic.

There can be no doubt that we are here concerned with an idea which is very important for the critical philosophy. Kant himself expresses it with unusual emphasis. He maintains that it is only because earlier philosophers have failed to recognise the synthetic character of mathematical propositions that no fruitful metaphysics has thus far been developed. It was for the same reason that even the possibility of a genuine metaphysics had been denied by Hume. Kant's view of mathematics is one of the cornerstones upon which he built his philosophy of a phenomenal world generated by constructive logic (cf. also commentary to Kant's 'Introduction' VI).

1. Before turning to the explanation proper, we must draw attention to a terminological difficulty. Kant here differentiates between (1) mathematical conclusions [*Schlüsse*], (2) mathematical principles and propositions

[*Grundsätze und Sätze*], and (3) mathematical axioms [*vorausgesetzte Grundsätze*]. Mathematical conclusions, as conclusions, are of course analytic. Mathematical principles and propositions are synthetic—more precisely, synthetic *a priori*. Finally, mathematical axioms, although analytic, only become real, only become applicable judgements, when they are manifested in the synthetically determined forms of intuition.

Kant's first example is the arithmetical equation $7 + 5 = 12$. In what sense can this equation or proposition be understood as synthetic?

According to Kant, an arithmetical operation is based on the fact that a logical principle (the principle of synthetic unity) is imposed on an indeterminate manifold. Kant therefore regards the number $(5 + 7)$ from two points of view: (1) as a unity (to be represented in space); (2) as a logically quantitative principle—the principle, namely, of the arithmetical series contained in the category of quantity.

The equation of the two points of view is possible through the medium of time. The medium of time is given as an indeterminate succession, and is determined by the understanding as ordered succession within which $5 + 7$ is a determinate point, 12. That is to say, the understanding produces the concept 12 by construing the two unities, 5 and 7, as a new and necessary unity in an infinite (and otherwise still indeterminate) series.

Similarly, the basic principles of geometry, and (even more so) the propositions, may be understood as synthetic. For example, a straight (i.e. the shortest) line can be construed as space determined in accordance with a logical principle, and that in the following sense.

The spatial unity of a straight line is simply a succession (an infinite number of points) manifested in space. The concept of the shortest line is the concept of a line with the smallest number of points, i.e. succession determined as an arithmetical series.

Kant describes a straight line from two points of view:

(1) as a spatial phenomenon; (2) as a logically synthetic unity. The medium in which the two points of view are united is time. For, by operating on an indeterminate succession (i.e. an indeterminate number of points in a straight line), the understanding generates the concept of determinate succession. That is, the understanding generates the concept of a series, in which one unity necessarily succeeds another; hence, the series is so determined that it contains a smaller number of points than any other (retrograde or irregular) movement. In short, an arithmetical series, $n^a \ldots n^b$, intuited in space, is a straight line. An arithmetical series $n^a \ldots n^b$, understood as quantitative unity, is the line containing the smallest number of points, i.e. the shortest line.

It is in this sense, then, that it is possible for Kant to describe mathematical propositions as synthetic. These ideas, which are so important for Kant's whole system, may be summarised as follows: (1) mathematical propositions are logical principles realised in the pure forms of intuition, space and time; (2) these logical principles are constructive in character; (3) a logic not manifested in space and time is empty.

Let us now turn to what Kant has to say about axioms, or the basic principles universally presupposed. Axioms, in contrast to principles and propositions, are analytic: they do not contain within themselves the formation of a new concept. The axiom is nothing other than the mere statement of identity, i.e. the basic logical principle applied to the concept (nature) and known as the law of contradiction. However, in traditional logic the axiom asserts the identity of the *given* concept; in the critical philosophy it states the identity of the concept *formed* by an act of synthesis. Thus, according to the critical philosophy, the axioms $a = a$ (the whole is equal to itself) and $(a + b) > a$ (the whole is greater than any of its parts) say nothing more than that the construction of the phenomenal world is valid. That is to say: according to the critical philosophy the axiom $a = a$

is nothing other than the concept of synthetic unity or the (empirical) concept in general, understood as validly (objectively) and thus identically constructed. Consequently, one may say of the axiom that, to be intelligible, it must be manifested in space and time; and that in itself it would be a mere 'ought' completely without content. In other words, the representation of determinate space and time must be given to us for the axiom to become real and have reference. Were this not the case, the axiom would remain a mere postulate of thought, neither intelligible to us nor applicable as judgement.

Thus Kant is here suggesting that the axiom $a = a$, from which the law of contradiction is derived, is intelligible only in connection with phenomenal reality or in connection with the logic of construction, i.e. with human thought;[3] and consequently that even this principle is something 'imposed' by the understanding, is a human presupposition of all knowledge. It is true, Kant maintains, that the law of contradiction is as necessary and immutable as the categories themselves;[4] yet by relegating it to a logic, which is applicable to phenomena only, Kant pointed the way to a most radical and perhaps never-to-be-completed revolution of logic. It has often, with justice, been emphasised that the logical side of Kant's philosophy has proved to be the most important and influential aspect of his thought. In order to carry on the logical revolution he began, his successors called in doubt the necessity of the categories upon which Kant himself had insisted.

2. Whereas Kant's theory of the synthetic character of mathematical propositions is treated in detail here in the first part of section V, the second and third parts of this section merely intimate ideas that are fully discussed only in later chapters.

The proposition 'that in all changes in the physical world the quantity of matter remains unchanged', is treated in the

[3] See also the commentary to the chapter 'Phenomena and Noumena'.
[4] A 150/B 189.

first Analogy (in this connection see also the 'Synopsis'). The proposition 'that in all communication of motion action and reaction must be equal to each other' points to § 5 (cf. the commentary to this section). Here Kant only briefly discusses the first of the quoted propositions. He looks at the concept of (formed) matter from two points of view: (1) of materially filled space; and (2) of logically synthetic unity. The union of the two points of view is made possible through time.

Matter filling space can be described in two ways: (1) as an indeterminate succession of representations; (2) as synthetically determined time; i.e. as something enduring as a whole with all its co-existent parts. Thus the act of understanding, in transforming infinitely given time into a unity, determines matter filling time as quantitatively unchangeable. In other words, the amazing certainty of our knowledge that empirically immeasurable matter never changes in quantity is based on the synthesis of time given *a priori*.

3. Finally, Kant implicitly distinguishes his own metaphysical theory from traditional metaphysics. He describes (traditional) metaphysics as, in intention at least, a science based on synthetic propositions, i.e. as constructive knowledge. In offering this account, Kant suggests that his own metaphysics—which admittedly he calls not metaphysics but transcendental critique—is arrived at, not by constructive-synthetic thought, but by clarificatory-analytical thought. This description of his own philosophy anticipates one of its chief consequences: namely, that traditional, system-building metaphysicians were crassly mistaken in supposing that they possessed transcendent knowledge. The knowledge and the concepts which they took to be pure and thus transcendent in fact involved space and time—or at least time. Their knowledge and concepts belonged therefore to sensibility. In short, according to Kant both constructive metaphysics and a metaphysics transcending sensibility are impossible. It implicitly follows that the only

genuine and fruitful metaphysics must be a critical or transcendental investigation based exclusively, as Kant assumes, on analysis.

SECTION VI

Résumé

Let us formulate the critical problem as the question: how are synthetic *a priori* judgements possible? This formulation is comprehensive; it involves the questions (1) how is pure mathematics possible? and (2) how is pure natural science possible? The answer to these questions will also show why traditional metaphysics has never been able to prove itself a true branch of human knowledge.

On the other hand, the desire for metaphysical knowledge is innate in man. As a result, we must raise the questions respecting metaphysics: (1) How is metaphysics as a natural inclination possible? (2) How is metaphysics as a science possible (since it has been shown that there cannot be a metaphysics based on synthetic *a priori* judgements)? This last question, however, contains these further questions: What is the value of the critical philosophy? In what does its peculiar nature consist? What is its method?

Explanation

Having described his work as an investigation into the foundations of knowledge (Kant's 'Introduction' III), Kant now poses the critical problem in the form in which it has become so famous: how are synthetic *a priori* judgements possible? Kant gives *part* of the answer at the end of the 'Transcendental Aesthetic' (cf. commentary to Kant's 'Conclusion to the Transcendental Aesthetic'). The complete answer, however, is contained in the section 'Of the ultimate principle of all synthetic judgements' (A 155/B 194; in this connection, see the commentary to the 'Transcendental Deduction', especially §§ 26 and 27).

The mistakes of all earlier philosophers, says Kant, are

based on the fact that they did not see the problem which he has posed. Failure to recognise that there are synthetic *a priori* judgements, that logic is constructive and that nature is a logically organised phenomenon must lead to a denial of the scientific character, not only of metaphysics but also of mathematics and pure physics. If Hume had realised that mathematical propositions are synthetic, he would never have fallen prey to a scepticism destructive of all pure philosophy (i.e. of all philosophy relating to what is necessary and universal). (On Kant's relation to Hume, see the commentary to §§ 19 and 26.)

What is it that makes the concept of the synthetic *a priori* judgement so remarkable and important? It is by means of this concept—or rather, the twin concepts of synthetic *a priori* and analytic judgement—that Kant is able to bring the whole field of human knowledge and thought, namely mathematics, (pure) natural science and metaphysics, under *one single* principle or question. Kant describes the propositions of mathematics and pure physics as synthetic *a priori* judgements; mathematics and pure natural science he therefore regards as logic applied to space and time. In adopting this position, Kant raises the question: can logic be applied to logic or pure thought to pure thought? As is known, he denies this possibility, and in making the denial also excludes the possibility of a metaphysics that is both synthetic and scientific. The question whether logic can be applied to logic or pure thought to pure thought thus contains the suggestion that the critical philosophy will present an entirely new kind of metaphysics: one based exclusively on analytic judgement combined with inference. (cf. A 722/B 750. 'A transcendental proposition is synthetic knowledge deduced by reason.')

Kant's work may, therefore, be described as an attempt to turn metaphysics into a science, i.e. into applied logic, here used purely analytically for the purpose of investigating the foundations of synthetic or constructive thought as it occurs in mathematics and the pure natural sciences. At the same time it determines the limits of fruitfully constructive thought and thus becomes a science of the conditions of the possibility of knowledge, i.e. it becomes a transcendental critique.

The first two questions (about the possibility of mathematics and the pure sciences) are answered in the 'Transcendental Analytic'. The third question (about metaphysics as a natural disposition) is the object of the 'Transcendental Dialectic' (cf. the 'Synopsis'). With respect to this third question, we may say this much here: the ultimate foundation of our metaphysical searchings lies in the limitations to which our powers of knowledge are subject. Whereas our intellect as reason is able to postulate real unity, as understanding it can only think synthetic unity (cf. commentary to the chapter 'Phenomena and Noumena'); and whereas our intellect as reason (as the faculty of inference and the source of the moral law) is potentially free from the conditions of our sensibility, as understanding it is totally subject to those conditions. Our never-ending search for metaphysical knowledge is thus based on the very constitution of human nature: it contains the divine, but with an admixture of the lower, sensible elements. Our restless quest for metaphysical truth is thus based ultimately on the fact that our intellect is not intuitive, that our faculty of knowledge is split in two.

In the penultimate paragraph of this section Kant makes a further intimation about the character of the 'critique' or scientific metaphysics he proposes to develop. His new philosophy will not be concerned with the endless multiplicity of illusory 'objects' (i.e. concepts) of reason, but only with the limits of our cognitive powers and the conditions of the possibility of validly constructive thought. It follows that Kant's own philosophy will itself be clearly limited and systematically finite in character.

Finally, and with splendid self-confidence, he rejects all earlier metaphysical systems. He once more emphasises that a genuine metaphysics is indispensable to human reason and expresses the hope that he will succeed in establishing a healthy and truly fruitful metaphysics by means of a new and completely revolutionary method.

SECTION VII

Résumé

The new metaphysics envisaged by Kant is to be called a critique of pure reason. Reason is here understood as the faculty which infers the presuppositions of objectively constructive thought. Pure reason, however, is understood as the faculty which (1) infers the presuppositions underlying the construction of original synthetic unity and (2) postulates absolute transcendent unity.

The critique of pure reason—which must be distinguished from the system of pure reason, i.e. a system consisting of all the *a priori* concepts hierarchically ordered —is, accordingly, an investigation into the pure knowledge accessible to us (i.e. the knowledge originating within ourselves). It thus also consists of an investigation into our cognitive powers, with the ultimate intention of determining the precise limits of the knowledge attainable by us.

Explanation

In the final section of the 'Introduction' Kant explains the title of his work. The new scientific metaphysics, discussed in the previous section, can alone, he says, bear the name 'critique of pure reason'.

In what sense are the terms 'reason', 'pure reason' and 'critique' to be understood? Since Kant's explanation in this section is all too condensed, we shall have to draw on the introduction to the 'Transcendental Dialectic', in particular A 298/B 355 to A 309/B 366. Already in traditional philosophy, reason is the faculty of inference; ultimately it is the faculty of inferring the highest concept, that of substance. In the critical philosophy, too, reason is the faculty of inference. But since, according to Kant, even the highest concept is formed by synthesis, reason for him is the faculty of inferring the presuppositions of validly constructive thought (in Kantian language: the principles of *a priori* knowledge). These principles are (1) the law of contradiction; (2) the presuppositions underlying both the structure of the phenomenal world and, as a result, *a priori* knowledge, namely space, time, the categories and their combination in the synthetic unity of apperception. (Cf. the section 'System of all the Principles of Pure Understanding', A 148 ff./B 187 ff. See also the 'Transcendental Deduction'.)

Traditionally, pure reason is the faculty by means of which we discover ultimate unity (true Being). The knowledge traditonally aimed at by pure reason was transcendent in character. According to Kant, the traditional method of pure reason was spurious synthesis. The critical view of pure reason, however, is that it is (1) our faculty of inferring the conditions of synthetic unity as the elementary basis of pure constructive thought (in Kantian language: the principles of pure *a priori* knowledge),[5] (2) our faculty of postulating both ideal totality (real unity) and an ultimate non-material cause of all changes in the phenomenal world (see the 'Transcendental Dialectic', in particular A 405 ff./B 432 ff.; cf. pp. 222 ff.). Pure reason in the first sense is examined in the 'Transcendental Analytic', and pure reason in the second sense in the 'Transcendental Dialectic'.

Kant's intention is to create, not the system, but the critique of pure reason. He does not intend to produce an organon of pure reason. An organon of pure reason would be a means of discovering all *a priori* concepts and propositions as principles of *a priori* knowledge. A system of pure reason would be produced by a thorough and exhaustive application of the organon to its object; it would have to contain the totality of all *a priori* concepts, both primary and secondary, discoverable by pure analytic judgements and

[5] Reason refers to the forms of thought realised in our spatio–temporal nature; pure reason, however, refers to the forms of thought manifested in an intuition in general. See, in this connection, §§ 21 and 23.

inferences of reason, and it would have to present them and the *a priori* propositions derivable from them in their correct hierarchical order of dependence.

Kant does not intend to construct such a system, which would be the system of transcendental philosophy. (Incidentally, one of the secondary concepts which would have to be mentioned in such a system would be the concept of 'condition of possibility'. This concept is obscurely contained in the category of existence and can be derived from it by analysis. Hence Kant's assertion that his philosophy is based on analytic judgement; cf. §§ 16 and 17 and the commentary to these two sections.) Kant's intention is only to create the foundation for such a system. This he does by only discussing, apart from the forms of intuition, the elementary, not the secondary, concepts and propositions. He is thus not aiming at the creation of an organon but only at a canon of pure reason.

Traditionally, a canon (cf. A 796/B 824) contains all the rules relating to the correct use of one of our faculties. A canon of general logic relates to our faculties of analysis and inference. A canon of transcendental logic, however, relates to our faculty of forming original concepts; that is to say, in the critical sense, a canon of transcendental logic is a theory of the method of constructive thought or of pure understanding. Potentially, it is also a canon of pure theoretical reason. But since, according to Kant, constructive metaphysical thought is impossible, a canon of pure theoretical reason cannot in fact be created. A canon of pure reason can never be more than a methodology of pure practical reason, i.e. a means of discovering ethical rules.[6]

Trancendental philosophy or the system of (pure) reason must, therefore, be distinguished from the transcendental critique or critique of (pure) reason. And yet it is still possible to say that the two concepts are essentially the same. The critique of pure reason is identical with transcendental

[6] On canon and organon, cf. A 61/B 85. A canon is a means of ordering knowledge; an organon is a means of acquiring knowledge.

philosophy in so far as the former will contain all knowledge of primary importance, while the latter will be left with the task of acquiring only such secondary knowledge as can be derived with relative ease from the knowledge already established by the critique. In other words, the critical enquiry will be complete once the essential goal of transcendental philosophy has been reached, i.e. once the limits of possible knowledge have been established.

COMPARISON OF THE TWO VERSIONS A 12/B 25 In the first edition the definition of transcendental knowledge[7] is limited somewhat too narrowly to pure *concepts*; the revised definition of the second edition includes pure intuition. It is probable that when writing the first version Kant allowed himself to be led astray by the immediate context in which he was discussing the system, not the critique, of pure reason. The system of pure reason is concerned, of course, exclusively with *a priori* concepts, whereas the critique of pure reason has to concern itself with the given forms of intuition as well.

This alteration has led to certain stylistic inequalities. The term 'knowledge' occurs twice in the definition; as a result the expression 'such concepts' in the next sentence has no direct reference.

In the final paragraph of the 'Introduction' Kant (1) draws attention to the two main parts of the book and (2) reminds us of the fundamental distinction upon which the whole work is based: the distinction, namely, between sensibility (receptivity) and understanding (spontaneity); between matter formed and form forming matter. Now, since the pure intuitions of space and time constitute a third, mediating, element within the above distinction, Kant emphasises that he has decided to treat the two intuitions as the forms of outer and inner sense respectively from the point of view of 'receptivity' in the immediately following part.

[7] First edition: 'knowledge which is occupied . . . with our *a priori* concepts of objects in general'. Second edition: 'knowledge which is occupied . . . with the mode of our knowledge of objects in so far as this mode of knowledge is to be possible *a priori*'.

TRANSCENDENTAL AESTHETIC

SECTION I

Résumé

Nature, organised or to be organised, may be described in three ways: (1) as the representation of conceptual unity or conceptual relations; (2) as the representation of intuitive, i.e. spatio–temporal unity or spatio–temporal relations; (3) as a something to which our senses react in many different ways.

Transcendental logic examines nature as conceptual representation; transcendental aesthetic examines nature as intuitive representation. There can be no methodical treatment of nature as merely received by the senses.

Explanation

Space and what is found in space are given in outer *intuition*; time and what is found in time are given in inner intuition.

Phenomenal nature as synthetic unity or as unity composed of various representations is constructed or comprehended by means of the *concept*.

Matter in us reacts to matter outside us by means of *sensation*, that is, in so far as we are conscious of such a reaction.

Nature as intuition, i.e. nature as materially filled space and time (the object), is *given*. Nature as concept, i.e. nature as an object comprehended by constructive thought, is not given.[1]

---

[1] Even intuition or unity in space and time are not *merely given*. Even they involve spontaneity, since they also are formed *a priori* by the

Empirical intuition is concerned with phenomenal nature as materially filled space–time, i.e. as a spatio–temporal object.

A *phenomenon* is an experienced manifold, categorically formed by the understanding, intuited as spatio–temporal unity, and comprehensible as a unity under various concepts.

Matter is nature of which we are not conscious, i.e. nature thought of as unorganised.

Form is nature as organisation. Whereas matter is given from outside, form lies within us.

Pure representations relate to form, i.e. to nature as spatio–temporal or conceptual unity or as a set of spatio–temporal or conceptual relations.

The pure forms of sensuous intuition are the faculties which enable us to represent nature as infinite space and time.

Pure intuitions are the pure forms of sensible intuition as intuited, i.e. nature as space and time, determinate or determinable. Space and time thus represent 'primary matter'. As form, this 'primary matter' first transfers its own characteristics, namely three-dimensionality and successive plurality, and then all the determination imposed on it by the understanding to 'secondary' or sensed 'matter'.

Let us now outline the argument of this section.

Wherever we try to acquire knowledge, our knowledge must always relate to unities and these unities must be given to us through the senses. Now, what we call unity can always be regarded as synthetic unity or as unity composed of unities. We say that we have knowledge of some unity or other only when we are able to grasp it as synthetic unity.

Both the immediate awareness of a unity and the unity itself will be called intuition. The act by which a synthetic unity is thought is called an act of understanding. The word

---

synthetic act of the understanding in combination with productive imagination. What is *merely given* is, as the 'Transcendental Deduction' most clearly shows, nature as a spatio–temporal infinity (or more precisely, a spatio–temporal indeterminacy) to which our senses react in various ways.

'understanding' will be applied exclusively to the faculty by means of which we synthetically construct or synthetically grasp a unity, i.e. to the conceptual faculty. Any concept can be regarded as a unity composed of unities or as a multiplicity of representations united together.

However, the impression which we receive through the senses may be described not only as a representation of (synthetic) unity but also as a pure manifold of sensations. For, as a being receiving impressions exclusively through the senses, we react to what is given merely by being variously affected. This is all that the senses by themselves can achieve. And yet a faculty inherent in the senses achieves more than this. I can have the *intuition* of a determinate unity, a figure in space, before the understanding *conceptually* comprehends this unity and determines it, say, as a line, cube or house. The faculty of intuition thus presents us with those unities, determined (in space and time), to which both our sensible impressions and our conceptual representations must refer. Since we are not self-creative any faculty inherent in us must always be formative, or bound to form. The question thus arises: What is the nature of the forms contained in our sensible intuition?

SECTION 2

Résumé

Whatever we intuit, or whatever our senses meet with, must occupy space or attach to occupied space. We may therefore describe all external relations as spatial and all objects as space; but space itself is the archetypal form of everything external.

Whereas formed concepts refer to what is particular and determinate, the original representation of space is universal; it is not formed but given; it is not determinate but indeterminate and determinable.

Explanation

KANT'S TITLE: 'METAPHYSICAL EXPOSITION OF THIS CONCEPT'
Kant distinguishes between 'metaphysical' and 'transcendental' and between 'exposition' and 'deduction'. An 'exposition' is the explanation of concepts which are both given and known, like those of space and time. A 'deduction' refers to concepts which are new and spontaneously generated, like Kant's categories. The intention of a deduction, as Kant himself says in § 13, is to prove the legitimacy of the spontaneously generated concepts. A 'metaphysical' investigation is related to the formal elements originally contained in our *determinate* representations of (1) unities in space and time; (2) the conceptual unity or (synthetic) unity in general. Finally, a 'transcendental' proof is intended to show that those formal elements are the means by which space and time, and thus the whole of nature, are originally determined. In short: the concept 'metaphysical' refers, in Kant, to what is originally determined in the phenomenon; the concept 'transcendental' to what originally determines the phenomenon.

FIRST PARAGRAPH In the first paragraph of this section Kant poses his problem and suggests a new solution to the question about the true nature of space and time. Earlier philosophers, the 'mathematical students of nature'[2] construed space and time as real entities. Others, like the Rationalists, 'the metaphysical students of nature', regarded space and time as determinations of or relations between things, and these determinations or relations they regarded as absolute properties. By contrast, Kant construed space and time as forms. He maintains that these forms, although subjectively contained in the human mind, none the less possess objective validity for anything we can regard as real.

In connection with Kant's theory of time, cf. the commentary to §§ 4 and 6.

[2] See § 7, paragraph 3.

TRANSCENDENTAL AESTHETIC

SECOND PARAGRAPH

1. We do not owe the representation of spatiality to the experience of different objects existing in different places. On the contrary: the representation of space is a condition of the possibility of our experiencing objects in different places. Indeed, the distinction between subject and object would be impossible without the underlying representation of space. I should be unable to relate the sensations called forth by matter *within me* to something existing *outside me* had I no representation of space in which sensations are first constituted as separate objects.

The critical concept of space is thus the exact opposite of the traditional notion. Traditionally, space is defined in terms of the objects existing in it. But for the critical philosophy objects are nothing other than materially filled space. It is through (determinate) space that they are first determined—indeed, first generated. Spatial qualities and relations cannot therefore be deduced either by observation or by thought: the qualities are given with consciousness and the relations are generated by the understanding by means of the categories.

THIRD PARAGRAPH

2. *First sentence.* If space is formative of intuited objects, it must be an indispensable condition of all our representations of objects. It is only because the manifold presented to the senses is intuitable as this or that spatial form that entities or objects can be formed for me at all. In short, a manifold as unity *is* a figure in space.

Second sentence. Although we can never think of material nature as non-spatial, we can think of space as not materially filled, i.e. as form.

FOURTH PARAGRAPH

3. If space were a discursive concept—if it were a concept based on the comparison of many different

representations of space and subsumed under the concept of spatiality—there would have to be many independent 'spaces', of which each would have to contain spatiality in general as its substance or inherence. But indeterminate space is one, and many different spaces are secondary parts of space determined through matter constructed as objects. It is thus not objects filling space that make different representations of space possible. On the contrary, the latter are based on the fact that space in itself is determinable (through the understanding).

It follows that geometrical propositions are not derived from concepts of determinate space—say, a triangle. They are not based, namely, on logical analysis, but on the original forming of space by means of the categories.

FIFTH PARAGRAPH

4. *First edition.* The representation of space further involves infinity. Representations of many spaces are always representations of limited spaces or measured distances (foot, yard). If the representation of space in general, as a discursive concept, were derived from representations of many spaces we should have the concept of measured space but not the representation of infinite space. Any conceivable object corresponds to determinate space; given space, on the other hand, is the infinite matter for all thinkable objects.

Second edition. Space is represented as an infinitely given magnitude. It is, of course, true that any concept derived from appearance, i.e. from determinate space–time, is thought of as infinitely determining (namely, for the objects subsumed under it[3]), but not as infinitely determinable. Such a concept rather signifies a unity of *determinate* representations or qualities—say, a rose. Infinity of qualities is the totality of all possible representations as unity, i.e. part of nature connected with all its other parts, or the infinite succession of time thought of as simultaneous. But

[3] Cf. 'Kant's reform of logic' II.

infinite multiplicity as unity is inconceivable for us; it can only be represented, and that as something infinitely determinable in itself: space, primary and given.

Comparison of the two editions. In the first edition Kant merely shows that space construed as concept can be finite only as far as its content is concerned. It is only in the second edition that Kant compares concept and intuition. He does so by proving that *infinite* content belongs only to pure intuition.

SECTION 3

Introductory

Kant now goes on to argue that (determinate) space is universally applicable, i.e. that it transfers the determination imposed on itself to the matter presented to the senses. Kant calls this part of his proof a 'transcendental exposition'. He offers a second, more detailed transcendental exposition of the concept of space in § 8 I, paragraph 7.

Résumé

Anything spatial, i.e. any unity of intuition, is divisible and measurable. The science of geometry concerns itself with dividing and measuring objects in space.

Only if we regard space as the primary matter in which the categories are manifested can we understand how geometrical propositions can be apodeictic. Geometrical propositions, namely, are based on the forming of space by original synthesis.

Furthermore, it is only by regarding space as the archetype of everything extended that we can understand how the laws of geometry can apply necessarily and universally to whatever is objective and externally intuitable (i.e. to materially filled space).

Conclusions

Respecting ourselves and our capacity for acquiring objective knowledge, we draw the following conclusions.

Spatiality, as the form-giving quality inherent in our sensibility, is both a faculty and a limiting condition. It is the faculty of intuiting what is extended, and that in measurable relations. It is the limiting condition which excludes from our intuition and experience whatever is non-extended and non-measurable. If we regard the thing-in-itself as something independent of the conditions of our sensibility, we shall have to concede that all our knowledge is limited to phenomena and cannot extend beyond them to things-in-themselves.

Explanation

TITLE AND FIRST PARAGRAPH Cf. commentary to the title of § 2.

SECOND PARAGRAPH Cf. résumé.

THIRD PARAGRAPH But how can space transform the manifold into objects? It can do so only in the following way: the primary matter inherent in our consciousness transfers its determination formatively to all secondary matter.

FOURTH PARAGRAPH Kant alludes[4] here to the theories of Newton, and Leibniz–Wolf. Their theories are deficient in so far as they are unable to explain the necessary character of geometrical synthesis. The critical philosophy, on the other hand, is able to offer an explanation. Kant goes into these theories in greater detail in § 7, paragraph 3, and in § 8 I.

Under the title 'Conclusions', Kant answers the question raised in the first paragraph of § 2: what is the nature of space?

FIFTH PARAGRAPH (*a*) Space, which forms the sensible manifold into objects (absolute determination) and creates the relations between objects (relative determination), is a form of *our* intuition and does not concern things-in-themselves. We must regard a thing-in-itself as a something

[4] The allusion is to the philosophy of Leibniz as popularised by Wolf.

TRANSCENDENTAL AESTHETIC

independent of the determining factors antecedent to its existence as a (synthetic) unity.

SIXTH PARAGRAPH (*b*) Space, as form inherent in us, is, so to speak, the 'intuitibility' or 'perceptibility' of whatever confronts our senses; in other words, space is neither substance nor inherence. This form determines the manifold given to our senses, i.e. imposes necessary unity and necessary relations on it.

SEVENTH PARAGRAPH As has been shown already, space relates only to the objects of our intuition. Thus unless we wish to assume that any understanding differing from our own—even the divine understanding—can only intuit or represent objects in space, can only intuit or represent objects as measurable synthetic unities; unless we wish to make this assumption we must admit that whatever we intuit or experience must be appearance.

Space is objective and real for us, to the extent that we must regard appearances in space as objective and real. In another sense, the representation of space is only ideal, for although space determines the objects of our intuition, space, once it is detached from the possible objects of our experience, is no longer real. It is nothing more than something thought, incapable of either attaching to things-in-themselves or of limiting a non-human intellect.

EIGHTH PARAGRAPH There is only one faculty related to what is external which is both subjective and yet objectively determining: the faculty of representing space. Other faculties inherent in us, like those of feeling and taste, lead merely to subjective sensations, and these, moreover, may vary from person to person. Such sensations may be described as subjectively real but not as objective nor ideal (since, in themselves, they cannot even be represented).[5]

NINTH PARAGRAPH Sensations, e.g. of colours and sounds,

[5] Although the first edition version is more explicit, it does not differ in content from that of the second edition.

are merely empirical. They are based on the particular constitution of the human senses and thus represent the reaction of matter in us to matter outside us. As a result, sensations do not afford us either knowledge of things-in-themselves nor even knowledge of appearances. They relate only to the matter of appearances, not to their necessarily and universally valid properties, viz. the forms by which they are constituted.

Kant does not, of course, here mean that we cannot know anything at all about colours and sounds, etc. But what knowledge we do have of colours and sounds, etc., is knowledge of quantities, degrees and causal connections. However, such knowledge presupposes objects in space and, as will be shown later, time determined according to the categories. In short: our sensations are related neither to forms nor to objects; what corresponds to our sensations is simply matter which is yet to be determined.

BASIC ASPECTS OF KANT'S THEORY OF TIME

Kant's theory of time is one of the most important parts of the critical philosophy; indeed, one might call it the foundation stone. Three points may be emphasised before we turn to the detailed explanation: (1) for Kant, time is the universal medium of both inner and outer nature; (2) Kant distinguishes between time as an indeterminately given magnitude and time as duration, simultaneity and ordered succession; (3) indeterminate time is given as the succession of the manifold representations referring to what is external.

It is this theory of time which makes it possible for Kant to prove that the human understanding legislates for nature. The human mind, he teaches, orders the indeterminate succession of its representations relating to materially filled space according to logical and categorical laws; it transforms given time into duration, simultaneity and ordered succession; it thus orders the whole of nature appearing in time.

And yet neither the view that indeterminate time is the

succession of our representations nor the distinction between indeterminate and determinate time is purely Kantian in origin. A similar view can already be found in Locke: 'We have our notion of succession and duration from this original, viz. from reflection on the train of ideas which we find to appear one after another in our own minds' (*An essay concerning human understanding*, book II, chapter 14).

Already according to Locke, then, time originates in the structure of our consciousness; viz. it is simply due to the fact that the multiplicity of our representations is successive. This distinction was taken up and developed by the English philosophers of the eighteenth century. Whereas Locke derives duration from succession, Richard Price already maintains that, although succession is of sensible origin, duration is not.[6] This already hints at the basic critical view that, while mere succession is a form inherent in our inner sense, determinate time is generated by the understanding.

Most of the accusations of self-contradiction and confusion levelled against Kant can be shown to be misunderstandings of Kant's theory of time. It is extremely important that this part of Kant's thoughts should be rightly understood; by its means do the 'Transcendental Aesthetic' and the 'Transcendental Analytic' form the unity that is the critical philosophy.

SECTION 4

Résumé

Anything real, whatever it may be, can be regarded as time; but time itself must be construed as a universally mediating representation, as the primary matter of the inner sense: the formative medium of all appearances.

We represent the parts of any object, taken by us for real, as co-existent; the changes we regard as states succeeding each other; the unity of the object we regard as duration in

[6] Cf. D. D. Raphael, *The Moral Sense*, Oxford, 1947, p. 124.

time. Whereas any determinate representation of something real is synonymous with time organised as duration, simultaneity and ordered succession, the whole of nature as something still to be known is synonymous with time, given and infinitely determinable in itself.

Explanation

1. Time is not determined by the parts or states of nature perceived by us at the same or different times. On the contrary: time (determined by the understanding) first produces the representation of a phenomenal world, consisting of co-existent parts and persisting through changing states, along with all the objects in it.

'*Einiges*' [here the word *Einiges* means 'what is one', viz. an 'entity'; in this context it does not mean 'several' or, as Kemp Smith translates, 'a number of things'] parts or states (1) as simultaneous, like the walls and roof of a house; (2) as successive, like water and ice. (Cf. commentary to § 26.)

2. If time is formative it is necessary. If time is the way in which we can have representations at all or in accordance with which we are only able to form representations, it follows that we cannot represent anything outside time. Although we are unable to represent material nature as other than temporal, we can think of time itself as nonmaterial, i.e. as form. This does not, of course, mean that we can know anything by a merely formal grasp of time (cf. § 22).

3. The axioms of time in general express the properties of both given and organised time. It has only one dimension (cf. § 6, paragraph 2); the modes of simultaneity and ordered succession are not only different from each other, they are actually contradictory (cf. § 5).

When Kant explains that these principles of time cannot be derived from experience, he is expressing the critical theory that the principles of simultaneity and ordered succession (both in the mathematical and physical sense) arise from the human understanding, and that it is through these principles that the pure manifold becomes unity, and succession permanence (for the latter is nothing other than a changing compound entity).

4. If time were a discursive concept, it would have to be based on many representations of time. But many representations of time are always determinate. Hence time as something to be determined cannot be a concept; it must be given. And yet given time can be represented as individual unity. As a result, such a representation can only be original, i.e. intuition.

A concept is based on the comparison of many particular representations of what is given and particular. Now, according to Kant, any empirical object—say, this flower before me—is space and time materially filled, i.e. empirical (secondary) intuition. But the original pure intuitions are space and time themselves.

Nor are the two representations of succession and simultaneity compatible under any concept (of traditional logic). The unity of these representations must, therefore, be based on the original forming of matter, viz. as nature (time) enduring through successive phases, with all its co-existent parts.

5. Time is given as infinite magnitude, i.e. as infinitely determinable in itself. What is given in this way, however, is the infinite matter for all determining concepts.

The second edition differs from the first in the last part of the fifth proof. The revision made here by Kant corresponds exactly to that in § 2, 4. First edition: 'since in their case the partial representations come first' means: the concept of a whole presupposes representations of determinate, i.e. synthetic unity. Second edition: 'since they [*scil.* concepts] contain only partial representations' means: *all* concepts are based on determinate representations, never on the infinite manifold. Thus intuition and the concept in general are first contrasted in the second edition.

Kemp Smith (loc. cit., pp. 134–8) particularly criticises Kant's theory of time. This is 'the most vulnerable tenet in his system'; 'there are five points which Kant has left unsettled' from which we may infer 'how greatly Kant was troubled in his own mind by the problems to which his doctrine of time gives rise'. Throughout this commentary I have tried to show that Kant clearly and consistently solved the problems connected with his theory of time. But perhaps an explicit refutation of the frequently repeated objections would be welcome here. Referring to the passages B 67, A 177/B 219, A 182/B 226, Kemp Smith says (loc. cit., p. 138), 'To sum up our main conclusions. Kant's view of time as a form merely of inner sense, and as having only one dimension, connects with his subjectivism. His view of it as inhering in objects, and as having duration and simultaneity as two of its modes, is bound up with his phenomenalism.' The alleged contradiction is resolved when one remembers that one-dimensional given time is determined by our own spontaneity as duration, simultaneity and ordered succession. Kant's two allegedly contradictory assertions in fact contain in combination the novel and specifically critical view of time—one of the most crucial of Kant's ideas.

SECTION 5

Résumé

Knowledge of general mechanics is intelligible only on the assumption that time is a universally mediating representation.

In mechanics we are concerned with empirical objects which at one time are here, and at another time there, i.e. not here; in mechanics we are thus concerned with determinate space as existent–non-existent. But we can neither intuit existent–non-existent space (object), nor can we resolve the contradiction inherent in this representation by any concept of traditional (analytic) logic. The union of A and not-A is possible only through synthetic logic. Such a logic is based on the assumption of a universal medium, i.e. indeterminately given time, determined as duration and ordered succession. The possibility of mechanics, which according to traditional logic rests on a contradiction and thus remains unintelligible, can only be understood by equating the existent–non-existent object with something enduring through changing states; by equating the existent–non-existent object with permanent but passing time.

Explanation

In the first edition the transcendental exposition of the concept of time consists merely in the proof that the properties of time are original (determining). In the second edition Kant adds that determinate time coincides with the axioms of mechanics or is at least expressed in them; and hence that determinate time contains the basis of a special science.

The important point about this subsequently added § 5 is this: Kant reveals here the basic deficiency of both traditional metaphysics and traditional logic. Both in the logical and in the metaphysical sense, traditional philosophy is incompatible with science. The concept of being, and thus the opposition of being and not-being, is absolute for traditional metaphysics. Traditional logic totally excludes contradiction—in spite of the fact that natural science is based on the concept of synthesis, of which the essence is the union of A and not-A (cf. also the commentary to Kant's 'Introduction' V, 1).

By contrast, (1) Kant shows that in order to explain the scientific knowledge which we are able to acquire we need the concept of being and non-being; that, as a result, both concepts must be regarded as belonging to phenomenal reality and that both are based on time and signify determinations of time; (2) Kant maintains, concerning logic, that a universal representation may be assumed, namely time; and that the opposition between A and not-A is resolved in this representation. In presenting these views, Kant is hinting at his logic of construction. This logic is alone compatible with natural science, for it alone is not dependent on what is determinate and given; rather, it constructively determines an indeterminate. In this it is, of course, bound to certain forms (the categories, determinations of time) (cf. 'Kant's reform of logic' II).

To show the kind of proposition Kant was here thinking of, we may quote the following passages from his *Metaphysischen Anfangsgründen der Naturwissenschaften*:

> Any movement, regarded as an object of possible experience, can be described in one of two ways: as body moving through motionless space, or as space moving at the same velocity in the opposite direction with the body at rest.

> The combination of two movements of the same point is conceivable only if the first movement is represented as being in absolute space while, instead of the second movement, a movement of relative space with the same velocity in the opposite direction is represented as identical with the first movement. [Part I, 'Phoronomy', principle I and theorem I]

These two propositions represent motion in general as the determination of pure space–time or, more precisely, as the determination of pure space by pure time. They are thus synthetic *a priori* judgements resulting from the application of originally determined time and space. By means of these propositions it is proved that a special science, mechanics, is possible only on the assumption that time is a medium or something both determinable and determining.

An inconsistency has been detected between § 5 and § 7, paragraph 4 (A 41/B 58), where movement is described as an empirical concept (cf. Kemp Smith, loc. cit., pp. 127f.). But Kant does not dispute the empirical character of motion either in § 5 or anywhere else in the *Critique of Pure Reason*. On the contrary, he says in § 5 that certain propositions referring to existent–non-existent space are *a priori* and that, since the empirical representation of movement is involved in the representation of existent–non-existent space, the above-mentioned *a priori* propositions are valid for all empirical movement.

TRANSCENDENTAL AESTHETIC

SECTION 6

Résumé

We can draw the following conclusions from what has been said so far:

(*a*) Time cannot be represented in itself but only as nature. On the other hand, time is not given with nature; nature is rather based on time; that is to say, matter first becomes the unity of nature through time.

(*b*) Time is given to us as the indeterminate succession of our representations; our determinate representations, however, which constitute our states of consciousness, are based on unified time. Time thus arises within us; hence time in itself has no describable form; it can only be described spatially, namely as one-dimensionality.

(*c*) Since there can be nothing external for me which is not an object of my representations, everything external is also something internal to or part of my consciousness. Now, any object I am capable of representing is something enduring, with all its co-existent parts, which remains the same through successive states. It follows that both outer and inner objects (unities) exist in time and are dependent on the laws of time.

Explanation

FIRST PARAGRAPH

(*a*) α: Time has no independent existence; as subjective form, time needs objective content. That is to say, my faculty for having successive representations would never become a representation of enduring time unless there were an object, determinate nature, to which my representations could refer. β: On the other hand, time cannot be derived from empirical nature as its inherence. On the contrary: the existence of nature as a unity presupposes time, i.e. the organisation of nature is, in a sense, nothing other than order in time.

53

SECOND PARAGRAPH

(b) Just as we cannot intuit the manifold as an external unity except by means of formative space, so is the unity within us only possible through the mediation of formative time. My determinate representations, which constitute the state of my consciousness, are based on time; on time is based the unity of my Self as the enduring subject of my successive representations.[7] In short: self-consciousness is, in a sense, identical with consciousness of time.

One-dimensionality is also a unique and thus primarily given representation which is conceivable only in terms of the spatial image of a line. The line presents time in all its aspects except one: the parts of the line are simultaneous; those of time are successive.

Thus Kant is here maintaining that we can only represent successiveness as applied, i.e. spatially manifested. When not applied, i.e. as empty time, it is a mere thought. But successiveness is the form in which multiplicity in general is accessible to us (cf. §§ 21–23); that we can only imagine formed multiplicity (successiveness) in the form of a line or in terms of a progressive numerical series (progressing, so to speak, in a straight line) is something inherent in the very structure of human consciousness; it is a condition imposed on us from the very beginning.

THIRD PARAGRAPH

(c) Mediately, time is the form of external appearances; immediately, it is the form of our inner states. It follows that time is the form of all represented objects. Time orders our changing representations (sensations) of what is external into an object, i.e. into a whole which, with all its parts, endures through different states. In short: the identi-

[7] Ultimately, this is possible through pure apperception, which, by means of the categories and operating as productive imagination, 'affects' the inner sense. Cf. the commentary of § 24, where Kant offers a detailed and definitive account of his theory of the inner sense.

cal objects appearing to us—the synthetic unities—are nothing other than filled time.

FOURTH PARAGRAPH Temporality, as a form inherent in our sensibility, is both a faculty and a limiting condition. It is the faculty of representing identical unities in the flux of sensations. It is a limiting condition which excludes from what we regard as real whatever we cannot represent as enduring with its parts through changing states.

We must, therefore, conclude that we are capable only of knowing appearances, not things-in-themselves. For unless we wish to assume that no understanding—not even the divine understanding—can grasp unities except as wholes whose parts are co-existent, whose states are successive and whose unity or identity is that of an enduring something—unless, then, we wish to make this assumption, we shall have to admit that what we represent as real is real only for us, i.e. that the reality of what we can experience is merely subjective. On the other hand, since whatever we represent is necessarily and universally determined by time, it follows that time possesses objective significance. In short: time is objectively determinative and determinate but only subjectively real.

FIFTH PARAGRAPH Time thus possesses empirical but not absolute reality. It also possesses transcendental ideality, since, although as our primary representation it is valid for all appearances, it exists neither in itself nor as part of something else existing in itself.

Finally, we must not forget what was said at the end of § 3 with respect to space, namely that there are no further determinative representations (faculties) other than the forms of intuition inherent in our sensible nature (cf. commentary to § 3, paragraphs 7 and 8).

SECTION 7

Résumé

FIRST PARAGRAPH In order to counter a possible objection,

we must add that the identical unity of the conscious Self depends, like any other appearance, on time, i.e. it is itself an appearance. We can infer from the fact of the changing states of my Self only what we infer from the fact of the changing states of all other identical unities: that time is real only in a subjective, not an absolute, sense.

SECOND PARAGRAPH Not to admit the ideality of time is to overlook the fact that there can be no subject for us without an object, and no object without a subject.

THIRD PARAGRAPH The very fact that the disciples of Newton and Leibniz construed space and time as substances or inherences, and not as forms, prevented them from explaining how our knowledge is arrived at.

FOURTH PARAGRAPH Space and time are the only two representations that can be regarded as undetermined and determinable, i.e. as primarily given.

Explanation

FIRST PARAGRAPH The objection unanimously (as Kant himself says) raised against the theory of the ideality of time runs as follows: my own representations are real; their changes are also real; change occurs in time; therefore time is real. The objection overlooks the fact that the identical unity of which I am conscious through all my changing stages, my Self, is itself, like any other object, made into a unity by time, and is therefore an appearance.

The objection is based on the first principle of Cartesian philosophy—the principle, namely, that consciousness involves the existence of the thinking Self. Like all his contemporaries, Kant accepted this principle. It is inferred that consciousness also involves the existence of the changing states of my Self and thus also the reality of my changing representations; finally, it is argued, these changing representations imply the reality of time.

Kant accepts both the original principle and the inferences which follow from it. But he maintains that the Self, consisting of changing states, is something represented and therefore dependent on time. According to Kant, it follows that time, although real, is only subjectively real (objectively valid). Since Kant thus admits the reality of time, while critically reinterpreting the concept of reality itself, he is able 'to admit the whole argument'—indeed he can use it as confirmation of his own theory.

SECOND PARAGRAPH The doctrine of the ideality of space is willingly accepted, while that of the ideality of time is generally disputed. Both doctrines, Kant suggests, are based on the Cartesian philosophy. For the Cartesians, external things are uncertain, but internal events, of which we are immediately conscious, are indubitably real. Against such a view Kant emphasises one of the crucial ideas of his philosophy: the idea that the object possesses reality only in relation to the subject, and the subject only in relation to the object; or, that matter which is real for us must be formed, and that form which is real for us must be manifested in matter (cf. commentary to § 16).

THIRD PARAGRAPH Kant now sums up once more the results of the transcendental aesthetic. He then continues: if one maintains that space and time are absolutely real, i.e. if one assumes that there are no mediating factors between thought and the reality of nature, it is impossible to explain how knowledge is arrived at. Newton and his successors regard space and time as absolute substances (although they have no independent existence) containing all measurable nature. Although this school of thought can explain the apodeictic nature and universal validity of geometrical propositions, it cannot explain our other—scientific—knowledge. The metaphysical concepts of this school of thought always imply space and time and are, therefore, not free from sensible elements.

The Leibnizians, on the other hand, regard space and time as abstractions derived, as inherences, from the objects of experience. As a result, they are unable to explain either

KANT'S THEORETICAL PHILOSOPHY

the apodeictic nature or the universal validity of geometrical propositions—though it must be remembered that anything relating to space and time is absent from their metaphysical speculations, which are based exclusively on pure logical forms.

Thus Kant rejects both a philosophy which construes space and time as ultimate sources of knowledge (space and time would then be 'non-entities') and a metaphysics which, as pure analytic, is dependent on the doctrine of pre-established harmony through its inability to establish a connection between thought and reality in any other way.

FOURTH PARAGRAPH Space and time are not merely the only two formative faculties inherent in our sensible natures, they are also the only two pure and thus originally determinable representations of our sensible natures. Any other representation—say, that of movement or change,[8]—presupposes a moving or changing object of experience and thus already determined matter. That is to say: there is no sensible representation which cannot be regarded as space and time or as a determination of space and time. But space and time themselves must be understood as the only all-embracing sensible representations.

SECTION 8

Introductory

The unusually long § 8 has no new conclusions to offer. Its purpose is rather to strengthen the critical theory of space and time from various points of view and to secure it against possible objections. It is a largely polemical section. In part I (A 41 to A 49/B 59 to B 66), which is the only part which appears in the first edition, Kant once more maintains the view against Leibniz–Wolf and Newton that space and time are to be construed neither as inherences nor as substances, but only as forms. In part II (B 66 to B 69) Kant

[8] Cf. the last paragraph of the commentary to § 5.

emphasises—probably in opposition to Mendelssohn—the phenomenal character of the Self as a proof of his theory of the ideality of time. In part III (B 69 to B 71) Kant explains that only appearances, not things-in-themselves, possess empirical reality. In doing so he emphasises the basic (and frequently misunderstood) difference between his own philosophy and Berkeley's theories that space and time are illusions. In part IV (B 71 to B 72) Kant explains, once more in opposition to Mendelssohn, that only the critical theory that space and time are subjectively real and objectively valid forms is compatible with natural theology, i.e. compatible with a rational concept of God.

SECTION 8 I

Résumé

FIRST AND SECOND PARAGRAPHS Kant's summary: empirical objects, i.e. determinate objects (synthetic unities) in space and time may be regarded only as appearances. What is not a synthetic unity in space and time, a thing-in-itself, is for us always indeterminate. Space and time are the determining media of empirical objects. Objectivity itself is nothing other than spatio–temporal order (in accordance with the categories, as is later explained). We cannot derive knowledge of things-in-themselves either from appearance or from space and time. For although we can intuit space and time, what we intuit is only the subjective form of our external or internal sensibility.

THIRD PARAGRAPH Those who assert that objects are given to us through the senses and that their thing-like elements can be obscurely felt and, as they hope, brought to light, assume that objects are determined by progressive analytic thought. But Kant maintains that all determinations of appearances are based on original synthesis, while things-in-themselves are always indeterminate for us.

FOURTH PARAGRAPH Thus, when Leibniz–Wolf connect or equate clarity with the thing-in-itself, and obscurity with empirical appearances, they are mistaking a merely logical–analytic distinction for a transcendental distinction. For whereas both clear and obscure thought may refer to concepts of reason, or appearances, or indeed even illusions, thought can never rise to the thing-in-itself. Appearance, whether grasped clearly or in a confused manner, must always involve forms.

Explanation

In the third and fourth paragraphs of § 8 Kant emphasises what is novel in his philosophy *vis-à-vis* Leibniz–Wolf. The latter, says Kant, make no distinction at all between the given and the determining. On the contrary, they assume that there is one single source of all knowledge—impure, it is true, to begin with, but capable of being purified. As a result, this school of thought thinks it is able to discover the pure form from what is given through the senses, that it is able to discover the thing-in-itself from appearances.

In contrast, Kant explains that if that which supposedly contains pure form is called sensibility, and that which supposedly contains thing-like elements is called appearance, then the concepts of sensibility and appearance become worthless. These concepts are fruitful only if the sensible is construed as what is indeterminately given and the appearance as what is determinately represented, if spontaneous form is opposed to sensible matter and the unknown thing-in-itself to knowable appearance.

Kant continues by maintaining that the distinction between clarity and confusion is purely logical. For knowledge of what is already determined, i.e. of what is already formed by original synthesis, and even the knowledge of valid moral concepts inherent in ourselves, is arrived at by progressive clarificatory thought; i.e. such knowledge becomes so much the clearer the greater the number of explicit judgements relating to it (cf. 'Kant's reform of logic' I).

Thus here, too, Kant is rejecting any philosophy which,

as mere analysis, not so much constructs a bridge between knowledge and its objects, as presupposes, without proof or justification, their (pre-established) identity. Kant regarded such a philosophy as unfruitful in both the metaphysical and the logical sense. It could not explain the possibility of our knowledge of nature; as pure analysis it involved a vicious circle (since it first determines reality according to the concept and then derives the concept from reality). As such, it must lead to dogmatism, conceptual jugglery and ultimately scepticism.

In contrast to the philosophy of Leibniz and his school, which Kant succeeded in supplementing, Kant's achievement may be assessed briefly in the following terms. By putting true being or the thing-in-itself beyond all human knowledge; by describing scientifically understandable nature as phenomenal reality validly, i.e. objectively constructed by the human understanding through the media of space and time; *by adapting thought to the unity of knowable nature*, Kant liberated his age from blind dogmatism and sceptical despair; he renewed philosophy—indeed, he awoke it from its slumbers.

SECTION 8 I *(continued)*

Résumé

FIFTH PARAGRAPH The critical philosophy, in contrast to the then current view, extends the meaning of the concept 'appearance' to include anything which is not determined in itself and whose determining factors we are able to name (because they are inherent in ourselves). Only that which is in itself determinate is to be called thing-in-itself. But we cannot think anything which is not first determined through space and time.

Explanation

In ordinary usage, the word 'appearance' refers to what may appear to our senses in various ways depending on their different natures. 'Object in itself' normally refers to what underlies the appearance.

However, what is often ordinarily called an appearance (say, the play of colours in a rainbow) is for Kant merely the matter of the appearance (cf. commentary to § 1 and § 3, paragraph 9); what is ordinarily called the object in itself is for Kant the appearance, i.e. matter already formed (the rain, or even the rainbow, as objects of knowledge). But the thing-in-itself lies beyond all appearance.

The *transcendental object* is the thing-in-itself.[9] In a sense we can say that this term contains within it, as it were, Kant's theory of the appearance and the thing-in-itself. For transcendental investigations do not aim at absolute objects but at object-creating subjective forms. But the objects we can know and which are dependent on the subjective forms cannot possibly be absolute. A transcendental object is hence an object which the critical philosophy will never investigate and which philosophy in general can never hope to discover. For the human understanding the transcendental object is a mere negative; only for a divine intellect could it be something positive.

As is known, Kant avoided using the term 'transcendental object' in the passages added to the second edition, without, however, removing it completely from the final text of the *Critique of Pure Reason*.

It is probable that while preparing the second edition he was particularly concerned with working out the positive side of his theory of the thing-in-itself, i.e. with describing the thing-in-itself as an object of the divine intellect. The object of the divine intellect is utterly and totally different from the objects of human experience and understanding. It has only *one* source; it is not a synthetic unity. It is probable that, while reflecting on the extent to which the

[9] Similarly H. Paton; we refer the reader particularly to his compelling refutation of the views of Vaihinger and Kemp Smith, who misinterpret the transcendental object as a category (Paton, loc. cit., pp. 421 ff.).

two senses of the concept 'object' are opposed, the term 'transcendental object' struck Kant as rather less than happy, since it obscures the difference between positive and negative noumena. Hence he removed the expression from those passages in which he was concerned with the opposition between negative and positive noumena, but he let it stand in those passages—and the present passage is one—where the unknown X may be understood in both senses: either as negative or as positive noumenon (cf. commentary to the chapter 'Phenomena and Noumena', especially p. 212).

SIXTH PARAGRAPH The second edition contains a reference to § 3, where there is a rather condensed transcendental exposition of the concept of space. The words added here are intended to limit the meaning of the following proof (§ 8 I, paragraph 7) which refers exclusively to space and geometry; in the first edition it is the definitive proof of the 'Transcendental Aesthetic'. In the second edition Kant adds new proofs of the ideality not only of space but also of time (§ 8 II–IV).

Résumé

SEVENTH PARAGRAPH The synthetic but apodeictic character of geometrical propositions can be explained only by the fact that space (and time) are media; the properties, synthetic and apodeictic, would remain unintelligible were it not possible to describe nature from a certain point of view (spatio–temporal) as both determinable and determining. If space were merely determined, then geometrical propositions would admittedly be synthetic; but they would then be various only in form, re-presenting what was determined and never apodeictic or necessary and universal. On the other hand, they could also be apodeictic but then they would be analytic, resolving what was already formed and thus synonymous with only *one* concept.

Thus it is only because space and time are determinable

in themselves (through the understanding in accordance with the categories) and determining (for nature) that we can understand how geometrical propositions can be both synthetic and apodeictic.

That is to say: geometrically ordered nature is nothing other than space–time logically determined.

Explanation

The 'object of outer intuition' is the logical form or relation realised in spatio–temporal nature as geometrical figure.

In connection with Kant's theory of the synthetic character of geometrical and arithmetical knowledge, see the commentary to Kant's 'Introduction' V, paragraph 1.

A COMPARISON OF KANT'S PHILOSOPHY WITH CERTAIN GREEK VIEWS, AND IN PARTICULAR WITH ARISTOTLE'S 'METAPHYSICS'

The full significance of Kant's theory of space and time will best be appreciated, it seems to me, if one compares the transcendental philosophy with certain Greek views, and in particular with Aristotle's *Metaphysics*.

1. According to Aristotle, pure form may be regarded as true Being, whereas matter, in and for itself, does not exist: only when it receives form does it participate in being. Matter is transformed into individual entities by universal form. It is these individual entities which possess Being. But only the pure divine form has full existence.

Kant is not satisfied merely to free absolute Being from matter; he separates it from form as well. He maintains that we know nothing of existent divinely creative form. On the other hand, he accepts the idea that mere matter by itself does not exist for us; that is to say, he maintains that whatever is real for us involves a combination of matter and form. Now, since phenomenal reality is a possible object of knowledge for us, it follows that, although the existent creative form is beyond human rational thought, form combined with matter can be described. Kant, as will emerge later, understands form as spontaneous logical form.

According to Plato, true Being belongs only to the ἰδέαι i.e. to general forms. Individual entities are formed in accordance with the ἰδέαι. Ideas exist in and for themselves; entities are merely their copies or shadows.

While rejecting the independent existence of such forms, Kant adopts the doctrine that matter is formed into individual entities by general forms. He concludes that individual entities and general forms are indissolubly connected, and that our knowledge of individual entities involves knowledge of such forms. Kant, while adopting the Aristotelian and Platonic views on form, does not regard the universal form as a class concept of general forms; in other words, he does not conclude that the universal form contains general forms within itself. He rather assumes that the universal form and general forms are to be distinguished, even though they are indissolubly connected in all our experience. Kant assumes that they, for their part, are related as form and matter.

Thus instead of the basic traditional dichotomy of matter and form (with an infinite number of mediating factors) Kant introduces a basic trichotomy. He assumes that between pure form and pure matter there is a mediating factor, an element that is matter for pure form, and form for pure matter. He assumes that space and time are matter for pure form, and immediate form for pure matter; that the universal form manifests itself in time and space as e multiplicity of general representations, while space and tima as general forms shape the manifold which fills them into individual entities.

2. In order to explain the relation of thought and reality, Aristotle appears[10] to assume that there is a definite hierarchy ranging from the highest form to pure non-existent matter, with an infinite number of intermediate formations in between. Just as the highest form moves matter by means

[10] W. D. Ross, *Aristotle*, London, 1923, pp. 167 ff.

of the intermediate forms, similarly thought must proceed syllogistically from the highest entity or the highest concept, arrived at by abstraction, to complex reality, or, *vice versa*, it must proceed from complex reality to the presupposed form. All syllogistic thought thus involves the assumption of true Being; and the truth or necessity of a valid syllogism, by means of which knowledge is inferred, is based metaphysically on the fixed order of the presupposed intermediate forms.[11] It would follow (since thought corresponds to pure form and consequently Being) that we should be able to derive reality in all its complex fullness by process of valid thought. That is to say: the theory of the stratification or fixed order of reality could lead to the view that all knowledge was analysis or rational inference from a divinely given universe.

Kant, however, makes it his task to free thought not only from the metaphysical concept of pure form or absolute substance but also from the assumption of a predetermined order of all things, while still retaining the concept of necessity indispensible to the idea that nature conforms to law. Thus instead of assuming that nature can be known through an infinite number of syllogisms, each one of which mirrors being, Kant maintains that nature can be fundamentally known through a single syllogism or operation of thought, namely: category → intuition → matter.[12] As a result, if the comprehensive syllogism is regarded as necessary, thought within each syllogism may be understood as free, i.e. as starting from experience but no longer metaphysically predetermined.

Kant's achievement may be described in two ways:

1. Kant wins for logic a new sphere of application. He does so by reinterpreting Aristotle's metaphysical con-

[11] Cf. W. Jaeger, *Aristoteles*, Berlin, 1923, pp. 407 f.

[12] Intuition: material nature (Transcendental Aesthetic). Category: intuition ('Metaphysical Deduction of the Categories'). Category: material nature ('Transcendental Deduction of the Categories').

cept of pure form in the sense of transcendental logic as category, on the one hand, and as natural law, on the other.
2. By means of his concept of a single medium, intuition, Kant saves scientific research from the paralysing assumption of a predetermined order of things and thus from degenerating into mere analysis. Intuition, which refers immediately to matter, may be filled with infinite content. As a result, it is only the basic law which is predetermined; all particular knowledge can be freely acquired through experience.

In this way, the famous critical synthesis is based on the concept of ideal intuition. It is through this concept that rationalism and empiricism first find their fulfilment.

SECTION 8 II

Résumé

Anything we intuit externally is equivalent to spatial relations; anything we intuit internally is equivalent to temporal relations. Hence not only the unity of nature which we represent to ourselves but also the unity of the Self are mere appearances, not things-in-themselves.

The inner sense, by means of which we intuit our Self, is given to us as an indeterminate succession of representations, i.e. as indeterminate time. And although we are originally conscious of the identity of the Self as spontaneity, yet the content of our representations of the Self is based on determinate time representations (states of consciousness) relating to what is external, i.e. organised time. But since the organisation of time is the product of our own spontaneity, it follows that the Self which we represent is based on the mind affecting itself, i.e. the Self we represent is merely appearance.

Explanation

This and the two following sections first appear in the second edition. The main intention is to prove the ideality or phenomenality of time and the Self and to do so as conclusively as was done for space and external nature in the previous section.

The problem of the phenomenal Self, intuited through the inner sense, is definitively treated in detail by Kant in the 'Transcendental Deduction' of the second edition, particularly § 24 II. I refer the reader to the commentary on this section. At this stage I merely add the following comments by way of clarification of particular points.

First and second sentences. The intuition of an object is the intuition of determinate space; the intuition of a moving object is the intuition of space being successively determined. It follows that our knowledge of moving or changing objects is merely knowledge of spatio–temporal determinations; it is not knowledge of the true nature of objects (as things-in-themselves), nor is it knowledge of the true and absolute nature of 'change'.

Textual: second sentence. 'What it is that is present in this or that location, or what it is that is operative in the things themselves apart from change of location, is not given through intuition' (*Was aber in dem Orte gegenwärtig sei, oder was es ausser der Ortsveränderung in den Dingen selbst wirke, wird dadurch nicht gegeben*). I omit the *es* (as Kemp Smith does) and construe *wirke* ('is operative') in the sense of *vor sich gehe* ('happen'). There is, namely, no possible concept to which *es* can significantly refer (since the first *was* ('what it is that') is indeterminate); the *es* after the second *was* ('what it is that') cannot be merely phraseological.

SECTION 8 III

Résumé

When the critical philosophy describes objects as appearances they are construed as real, even though they are dependent on subjective forms; they are certainly not to be taken for illusions. The critical theory is not to be confused

TRANSCENDENTAL AESTHETIC

with Berkeley's view that objects are merely illusions. It is understandable that Berkeley was unwilling to accept the absurd theory that space and time are properties of things and yet also independently existing magnitudes. But Berkeley's own theory is no less unacceptable. The untenability of Berkeley's own theory is most clearly shown by the unconceded but none the less inevitable conclusion that our own existence is merely an illusion.

Explanation

Second sentence [*second and third sentences*]. 'Since, however, in the relation of the given object to the subject, such properties depend upon the mode of intuition of the subject, this object as *appearance* is to be distinguished from itself as object *in itself*.' Kant is by no means saying that a thing-in-itself corresponds to every appearance or that every appearance is specifically related to a thing-in-itself. Kant is rather comparing the concept of 'appearance'—which, unlike the concept of 'illusion', involves the moments of reality and objectivity—with the concept of the 'object' or 'thing-in-itself'. Whereas the thing-in-itself exists independently and determinately, the appearance is dependent on its forms which first make it into an entity. Kant is not slipping into naïve realism here (as has been alleged); on the contrary, he is emphasising as strongly as possible the distinction between his own view of the object and that of the naïve realists.

'It would be my own fault, if out of that which I ought to reckon as appearance, I made mere illusions, *scil*. by regarding as absolute what is perceived through the senses' (cf. commentary to Kant's footnote, below).

Last sentence [*penultimate and last sentences*]. The conclusion that our own existence is merely an illusion (assuming that time were also merely an illusion) is altogether absurd, historically speaking, since it involves rejecting Descartes' first principle upon which the whole of seventeenth- and eighteenth-century philosophy was based.

KANT'S THEORETICAL PHILOSOPHY

Kant's footnote

Kant's intention is to show that only the critical view can enable us to understand how we can make objective judgements, or, to use his own words, 'can ascribe predicates to objects themselves', and that when the judgement is taken to refer to things-in-themselves illusion arises. The footnote thus contains the critical distinction between true and false judgements, both in the sphere of experience and in the sphere of metaphysics.[13] The distinction may be expressed as follows: true judgements about the properties of objects are possible only because we generate objects as spatio–temporal appearances; false judgements involve the view of objects as things-in-themselves.

We can make objective judgements only about appearances. If objects were things-in-themselves, i.e. were given absolutely or with absolute properties, then all our empirical 'knowledge' would merely be based on sense impressions (like those of Saturn and its two rings) and could therefore not be objective; on the other hand, all our apparently pure knowledge of reason would involve sensible elements (spatiality and temporality).

It is possible for us to have valid knowledge—pure or empirical—and thus make true judgements only because that which is determined by us in space and time as appearance is objectively determined or validly constructed. Illusion would arise, however, if we tried to make assertions about something which we had not ourselves constructed in accordance with the categories from spatio–temporal elements, and which did not therefore exist either as an object of our senses or as a thing-in-itself for us, or if we tried to make judgements about properties or spatio–temporal relations as if they existed independently of the objects to be constructed by us.[14]

[13] Kant's theory of error in general, *scil.* as possible content of consciousness, is presented in § 18; cf. commentary, pp. 155 ff., and also pp. 168 f.
[14] Kemp Smith, appealing to Vaihinger, sharply criticises this note

TRANSCENDENTAL AESTHETIC

Kant also treats the problem of false judgements in the first introductory section of the 'Transcendental Dialectic', though not with the sharpness and precision of the footnote just discussed. What Kant says in the introductory passages of the 'Transcendental Dialectic' may be summed up as follows. The understanding, by constructing spatio-temporally bound matter or the source of sensations, creates the basis of real knowledge. But in so far as the sensations occur as constructed, i.e. as already to a certain extent pre-constructed for the understanding which is applied to them, error—in proportion to the influence of the senses on the understanding—is unavoidable.

SECTION 8 IV

Résumé

FIRST PARAGRAPH Natural, i.e. rational, theologians try to construct a representation of God according to which he is free from all sensible limitations and thus from the conditions of spatiality and temporality. But it is nonsensical to maintain that God is independent of space and time while also maintaining that space and time belong to the existence of things. For the determining form of the absolute can only be the divinely creative. In other words: by attributing space and time to things-in-themselves God is made dependent on space and time.

But if space and time are forms which are not absolutely creative but only mediately so, they require created matter to manifest themselves; space and time are attached to what is given and must therefore be given.

SECOND PARAGRAPH Even if one assumes that space and

(loc. cit., pp. 148 ff.). Whereas Vaihinger detects two contradictory concepts of illusion here, Kemp Smith discovers three. But in fact, far from confusing heterogeneous concepts of illusion, Kant manages to condense the critical theory of false judgement into one short note.

KANT'S THEORETICAL PHILOSOPHY

time are valid for all created beings, space and time, in spite of such general validity, would still belong to what was given to sensibility. The only thing which is not given is what is spontaneously creative (both of itself and the universe), i.e. pure existence itself. But whatever is not self-creative is, from the point of view of its existence, dependent —dependent, that is, on phenomena and their mediating forms. These latter, space and time, must therefore be given.

Explanation

Kant finally shows that his theory of space and time is alone compatible with a rational concept of God.

FIRST PARAGRAPH Kant argues that God must be independent of space and time if what he knows (intuits, creates) is itself independent of space and time. It can be assumed that God created himself and the universe by becoming conscious of himself; that is to say, the originally creative and the originally created coincide. If space and time belonged to the absolute, God himself would be dependent on space and time—or, to give the idea an extreme formulation, space and time would themselves be God.

In connection with the concept of intellectual intuition and that of the positive noumenon as the object of divine intuition, see the chapter on 'Phenomena and Noumena'.

If space and time do not belong to things but only to created nature, they are given, and that as forms inherent in our sensible nature.

SECOND PARAGRAPH With reference to a sensuous but non-spatio–temporal intuition, cf. the commentary to the 'Transcendental Deduction' and in particular to § 23; cf. also the commentary to § 25 and § 24 II, in connection with the determination of my existence by means of time and objects in space and time, i.e. the forming of my particular existence which first enables me to know my Self as appearance.

CONCLUSION OF THE 'TRANSCENDENTAL AESTHETIC'

Introductory

The critical problem—how are synthetic *a priori* judgements possible?—is thus partly solved in the 'Transcendental Aesthetic'. One of the two factors which make such judgements possible has been discovered: pure intuition. The other factor, the pure concept or pure synthesis, will be worked out in the 'Transcendental Analytic' (cf. Kant's formulation of his final conclusion at the end of the 'Transcendental Deduction', A 158/B 197).

In connection with the synthetic *a priori* judgement, see the commentary to Kant's 'Introduction' IV. We may merely add here that the term is without doubt deliberately paradoxical.[15]

It is easy to understand that the original act of creation precedes the created world; one can understand that the complex created world is logically described by synthetic judgements. But when Kant speaks of a constructive *judgement* preceding the created world, he is being intentionally paradoxical. Kant formulates the paradox to

---

[15] Incidentally, an element of paradox is detectable in almost all Kant's terms. In this, Kant was following Rousseau, whom he admired so much. Thus form, which is abstract, is for Kant intuitable—indeed, it is the only possible object of pure intuition. For Kant the appearance is real; the thing-in-itself is a mere negative. Seen as object, Kant calls the appearance ideal; from the subjective point of view it is real. Even the title itself, *Critique of Pure Reason*, is paradoxical. What is beyond all critique, what, indeed, ought to be the very source of all critique, this Kant promises to make the object of the critique. Rousseau's famous paradox of the sovereign people both ruling and obeying itself, both bound and liberated by its own legislation, has its counterpart in each of Kant's three greatest works. The understanding legislates both for nature and itself by means of the category and it is inescapably bound by its own legislation. As practical reason I give both myself and all mankind the moral law; in doing so I both bind and liberate the will. Finally, genius both binds and liberates art in so far as he gives both himself and his successors aesthetic laws of form.

express with unmistakable clarity the idea that the act by which *man* creates the world is logical in character.

Résumé

Synthetic *a priori* judgements are possible because there are pure intuitions or media which, themselves determined by the understanding, determine the whole of nature. New knowledge cannot be derived from a single concept. A concept, e.g. that of a triangle, is derivative and contains itself alone. But the intuition of the triangle, i.e. space logically formed in accordance with the category of quantity, involves certain relations like the order or distribution of 180° through three angles. It thus makes possible the law that the sum of the internal angles of a triangle is constant.[16]

A synthetic *a priori* judgement is thus nothing other than the express description of synthetic relations or entities, originally created by our logical spontaneity in space and time—and thus valid for all appearances and yet only for these.

THE RELATION OF THE 'TRANSCENDENTAL AESTHETIC' TO THE 'TRANSCENDENTAL ANALYTIC'

The purpose of the 'Transcendental Aesthetic' is to show (1) that space and time are the matter which is primarily given to us, (2) that every determination of the original matter applies necessarily and universally to all secondary matter, to all matter empirically given to the senses, and thus to all appearances whatever.

Kant thus treats space and time in the 'Transcendental Aesthetic' first as given magnitudes and then as determining media. In the 'Transcendental Analytic' Kant shows how the indeterminately given forms of intuition originally receive their determinateness: namely, through the understanding in accordance with the categories.

[16] Cf. also Kant's own example from geometry in the 'Introduction' V—the law that the shortest distance between two points is a straight line. See the commentary to that section.

TRANSCENDENTAL AESTHETIC

In the second edition Kant throws further light on the relation between the 'Aesthetic' and the 'Analytic'. In the first footnote to § 26 (B 160 n) he says that, although in the 'Aesthetic' the unitary representations of space and time are merely treated as belonging to sensibility, without the co-operation of the understanding they would not be possible. Paton (loc. cit., I, pp. 123 f) has detected a contradiction here. In the light of B, 160 n, Paton finds it difficult 'to defend Kant's statement that space is represented as an infinite *given* quantity' (A 25/B 39).

But it seems to me that what Kant wishes to express in B 160 n, is the idea that in the 'Transcendental Aesthetic' space and time are treated as given unitary magnitudes, since they are presented to the consciousness as such, but that in the definitive treatment in the 'Transcendental Deduction' they must be construed as originally indeterminate elements, which are first unified by the understanding (cf. commentary to § 15).

There is also a difficulty attaching to Kant's use of the term 'given'. The expression 'merely given' means 'completely indeterminate'; but that which is *represented as given* is already determined—namely, by the understanding. In short: not even space and time can be represented as mere matter but only as formed matter, though—from the standpoint of the synthesis realised in the consciousness—space and time can be thought of as indeterminate.

TRANSCENDENTAL LOGIC

Metaphysical Deduction of the Categories

INTRODUCTORY

In the second main part of the *Critique of Pure Reason*, the 'Transcendental Logic', Kant is concerned with thought, i.e. the mind understood as the faculty of conceptual spontaneity, or nature regarded as conceptual relations. Kant's first intention is to discover the pure rules of thought (in the 'Metaphysical Deduction'). His second intention is to prove that the 'substance' of everything we represent—intuitively or conceptually—is identical with those pure rules of thought ('Transcendental Deduction'). Kant is then in a position to show that all our knowledge is limited to the pure rules manifested in the materially filled media (of space and time), and that any (theoretical) concepts exceeding these limits are illusory and deceptive. In this way, Kant presents his reader with his revolutionary philosophy which puts logic and metaphysics in a new relation, i.e. establishes a new metaphysics on the foundation of a reformed logic. But whereas Kant's novel metaphysics is intended radically to upset all previous metaphysics, his reformed logic, the logic of construction or synthesis, is not intended to render traditional logic superfluous. His reformed logic is intended to include traditional logic as a secondary or derivative logic capable of serving as an instrument of clarification and confirmation (though it is totally unsuited for creating knowledge outside the limits of experience).

TRANSCENDENTAL LOGIC

I. LOGIC IN GENERAL

Introductory

Since the ultimate object of the critical philosophy is thought, and since its real intention is to explain under which conditions or within which limits thought can lead to knowledge, Kant opens the second main part of his work by generally (1) determining the part which thought plays in knowledge; (2) expounding the science of thought, i.e. logic. With respect to (1) Kant shows—in the first two paragraphs of this section—that although all our knowledge involves thought it also involves something additional to and different from thought (for thought by itself is empty).[1] He thus regards the object from two points of view: (*a*) as something intuited and (*b*) as an object conceptualised and known; or to put it as Kant also puts it: the object is regarded (*a*) as something received by the mind and (*b*) as an object spontaneously thought and known by the mind. That is to say, Kant's basic distinction between organised nature and organising thought (between matter formed and form forming matter) emerges here as the distinction between intuited or given nature and conceptualised or known nature.

According to the critical philosophy, nature is nothing other than the product of the human mind, which logically determines given intuition, i.e. materially filled media of space and time. That is, knowledge of nature is based critically on *one* operation of the mind—an operation by means of which nature is simultaneously conceived and intuited. However, Kant is not yet prepared in the introductory paragraphs of the 'Transcendental Logic' to give an account of his theory, i.e. the result of his investigation. Here, as in the introductory paragraphs of the 'Transcendental Deduction' (§ 13), Kant is more concerned to prepare the reader for an account of his theory; he does so by posing the

[1] Cf. résumé in connection with 2.

problem. He distinguishes strictly between intuition and concept. By describing knowledge as the union of intuition and concept he implicitly poses the question: how is such a union—i.e. how is knowledge—possible?

Résumé

FIRST AND SECOND PARAGRAPHS Knowledge is composed of intuition and concept: just as in the 'Transcendental Aesthetic' we isolated intuition, made it the sole object of our enquiry and discovered certain rules inherent in it, so here, in the new science of transcendental logic, we can isolate thought and make it the sole object of our enquiry. We describe pure thought or the pure act of understanding as the operation by means of which some datum or other is coherently determined.[2] For, just as in the 'Transcendental Aesthetic' we construed nature as a pure spatio–temporal unity or as pure spatio–temporal relations, so here we can try to expound nature as a pure conceptual unity or as pure conceptual relations.

THE REMAINING PARAGRAPHS TO THE END OF THE SECTION The new science of transcendental logic is to be founded on general logic. We must, therefore, make it clear that it is not a particular branch of logic (the method of a particular science) nor so-called applied logic (psychology), but solely pure general logic alone, which can serve as a foundation for transcendental logic. For only general logic, which can refer to any kind of object, is exclusively concerned with the pure rules of thought.

Explanation

FIRST PARAGRAPH *First sentence* [*first and second sentences*]. If objective nature is represented as the matter given to and

---

[2] Coherent thought is understood in two senses: (1) as unity of conceiving, and (2) as logical consistency of reasoning; cf. Kant's distinction between the mathematical and dynamic categories. See commentary to § 11.

TRANSCENDENTAL LOGIC

formed by the mind, the mind itself can be construed as (1) receptive and (2) as spontaneously productive. If that which is received is understood not as merely unformed matter but as matter appearing in space and time, the given can be understood as the object of intuition, and the spontaneously productive or thinking mind can be understood as the knowing mind. For the act by means of which given nature, as the object of intuition, is thought or conceived is none other than the act by means of which objective nature is known.

'Representation' [*Vorstellung*]. This is Kant's most general term, which even includes conceiving (cf. A 320/B 376). Kant thus here adds the limiting term 'impression' [*Eindruck*] so that conceiving is excluded and 'representation' is limited to intuition.

'Object' [*Gegenstand*]. This term includes the unity of intuition and the synthetic unity of the concept, i.e. for conception it may be determinate or indeterminate. The object as given is intuited unity; as thought it is produced unity.[3]

'which is a mere determination of the mind' [*als bloße Bestimmung des Gemüts*]: accusative. The representation as impression is synonymous with the mind determined by the organised forms of intuition (of space and time), i.e. with the mind confronted by a given object [*Gegenstand*] but not conceiving or knowing the object [*Gegenstand*] objectively [*als Objekt*].

Second sentence [*third sentence*]. Knowledge of objective nature must always be described as the union of intuition and conception. For if the act by means of which objective nature is known is the same as the act by means of which a given manifold of representations is transformed into representations of synthetic unity via the media of space and time, then it follows that knowledge of objective nature

[3] Kant differentiates between *Gegenstand* and *Objekt*. In the latter, intuition and concept agree; it is the known or validly constructed entity.

is synonymous with the concept manifested in the materially filled media of space and time. That is to say: knowledge of objective nature is nothing other than the concept combined with intuition; knowledge of objective nature is based on the connection and agreement of concept and intuition.

The remainder of the paragraph. Furthermore, our concept of 'media' enables us to distinguish between empirical and pure intuition. For, whereas we describe the materially filled media as empirical intuition, we can call pure space and time (nature regarded as spatio–temporal unity or as spatio–temporal relations) pure intuition. Correspondingly, we can describe conception as either empirical or pure, depending on whether it relates to empirical or pure intuition. Pure conception can, accordingly, be defined as follows: it is coherent thought applied to a universal medium (e.g. space and time); in this way, it is made universally applicable, under the form of fundamental rules, i.e. the categories.

For an explanation of the terms used here, e.g. 'sensation', cf. the commentary to § 1.

SECOND PARAGRAPH *First sentence.* Sensibility includes the faculties of sensation and intuition, i.e. sensibility is the receptive mind in its relation to the matter which fills the (determinate) media. Spontaneity, on the other hand, is the understanding, i.e. the faculty inherent in us of generating (objective) nature, and also of conceptually determining it.

The remainder of the paragraph. Our human nature is such that intellectual intuition is denied to it. *Our* intuition—which is sensible in character—contains no other elements of objective knowledge than the two forms of intuition, space and time. Hence, whereas we can think of the Creator as not needing a separate faculty of understanding but capable of knowledge by means of intuition alone, for our kind of knowledge conception and intuition are equally

TRANSCENDENTAL LOGIC

indispensable. 'Thoughts without content are empty, intuitions without concepts are blind.' But, as Kant adds with great emphasis, the distinction between intuition and conception is of the greatest importance. Kant's reference to the significance of this distinction can be explained in the following way: although the unity of intuition is ultimately identical with the synthetic unity of the concept, the possibility of the critical philosophy is based on this distinction, by means of which the objective character of our spontaneous representations of nature can be proved. In other words, only in the light of this distinction is it possible to understand how nature can be both given and yet also spontaneously generated by the mind. By contrast, the empiricist must assume that nature and thought are merely given; the philosopher of the traditional school of metaphysics must assume that thought itself can lead to knowledge.

THIRD, FOURTH AND FIFTH PARAGRAPHS Cf. résumé. With reference to 'organon' and 'canon', cf. the commentary to Kant's 'Introduction' VII.

SIXTH PARAGRAPH Kant explains the new sense in which he uses the expression 'applied logic', i.e. a science concerned with the empirical sources of logical errors, like inattentiveness, etc. Ordinarily, applied logic meant logical exercises. But here Kant extends the meaning of the term to include what we today would call psychology. In extending the term in this way, Kant emphasises that there can be only *one* basic science, namely, logic.

II TRANSCENDENTAL LOGIC

Introductory

In order to characterise his new science of transcendental logic, Kant compares it with general logic. General logic understands unitary or coherent thought as a system of basic rules relating to already constructed objects. Transcendental logic construes such thought as an operation of the understanding, by means of which certain rules are realised—realised, that is, in space and time, i.e. as an operation by means of which objects are originally constructed.

Résumé

Thus we can reinterpret pure general logic as transcendental logic. We can do so by construing unitary thought not merely as a fixed determinate system of rules but as a determining constructive instrument of the understanding, i.e. by relating it to the pure manifold as its matter. It then follows that, unlike general logic, transcendental logic cannot completely dispense with its own peculiar content or object. Pure general logic determines neither space and time nor the phenomena of nature, though the concepts it uses may refer to both. Transcendental logic, on the other hand, is concerned with the original determination of space and time, i.e. with the manifold (as its own matter). As a result, transcendental logic is a science concerned with the origin of the pure conceptual forms of all objects.

Explanation

FIRST PARAGRAPH Kant once more defines general logic as a science of the pure rules of thought. He then continues: if it is possible to intuit nature both as a (material) phenomenon in space and time and as pure spatio-temporal relations, it will perhaps also be possible to *conceive* nature both as spatio–temporal unity and as spatio–temporal relations. That is to say: it will perhaps be possible to understand pure spatio–temporal relations as logical relations. In this case, says Kant, a kind of logic would become possible which was not completely independent of its object, nature; such a logic would be independent of nature only as an organised (material) phenomenon. Its object would necessarily be nature as a pure spatio–temporal infinity which has yet to be conceptually organised.

Textual. I transpose the word 'solely' or 'only' (*bloß*) and

TRANSCENDENTAL LOGIC

read 'This other logic, which should contain [solely] the rules of the pure thought of an object, would exclude only those modes of knowledge which have empirical content.' The position of the word 'solely' (*bloß*) makes no sense in the traditional position. It would make sense only if there were a branch of logic concerned with something additional to the rules of the pure thought of an object, but there is no such science. On the other hand, the word 'only' is indispensable after 'would exclude', since Kant wishes to emphasise that, although general logic is independent of the content of all knowledge, transcendental logic is independent 'only' of the content of *empirical* knowledge.[4] The new logic would concern itself with the rules of thought (concepts) by means of which nature is originally and spontaneously organised, while general logic is concerned only with such concepts as refer to already organised nature.

SECOND PARAGRAPH

Introductory. Although Kant characterises this paragraph merely as a 'remark', he also emphasises its far-reaching importance. He expressly warns us against confusing *a priori* and transcendental knowledge. Then, at the end of the paragraph, he explains in general terms that empirical and transcendental knowledge—a broader distinction which embraces *a priori* knowledge—refer to the same object, namely, nature known or yet to be known. However, while empirical knowledge is knowledge of organised nature, transcendental knowledge is based on the distinction between organising form and matter yet to be formed; that is to say, transcendental knowledge is synonymous with a critical theory of knowledge of organised nature.

Both the observations made here by Kant are certainly of far-reaching importance:

1 If transcendental knowledge were the same as *a priori*

[4] Adickes inserts *bloß* in the same position as I have done; but he does not delete it from the traditional position. [Kemp Smith adopts Adickes' reading in his translation.—*Translator*.]

knowledge, transcendental philosophy, like mathematics and pure physics, would be only an *a priori* science of organised nature, not a unique science of the organisation of nature by the understanding. On the other hand, if *a priori* knowledge were the same as transcendental knowledge, mathematics and pure science would be 'transcendental' or even transcendent sciences, i.e. sciences concerned with the origin of objects (or things) in general—a claim which Kant's philosophy is expressly designed to refute.

2 If transcendental philosophy were divorced from experience, it would itself be 'transcendent philosophy'. But the transcendental philosophy actually goes so far as even to assert that it can be corroborated and confirmed by juxtaposing its own theory with ordinary experience. Transcendental philosophy aims exclusively at the thorough investigation of the foundations of knowledge. Even though transcendental philosophy is new and unique, its doctrine must still be rather analytic and negative than synthetic and positive. In maintaining this position, Kant is emphasising that no discoveries about non-natural objects may be expected from his investigations.

First sentence [*first, second and third sentences*]. The only knowledge which may be called transcendental is not what we called *a priori* knowledge (e.g. mathematical propositions), but knowledge explaining the original character of space, time and the categories and thus the universal validity of the categories for all experience.

Textual. For purely grammatical reasons I transpose the word *transzendental* to read '... *oder möglich sind (das ist die Möglichkeit der Erkentnis oder der Gebrauch derselben a priori), transzendental heißen müsse*. It is possible that, when correcting the text, Kant added the words in brackets—and possibly *bloß* in the paragraph above—but unintentionally put them in the wrong place.

Second sentence [fourth sentence]. Although the representation of space and although geometrical knowledge are both *a priori* in character, they are not for that reason transcendental. Only the doctrine presented in the 'Transcendental Aesthetic' (explaining *why* geometrical knowledge is *a priori* and universally valid) may be called transcendental knowledge.

Third sentence [fifth sentence]. The doctrine of the 'Transcendental Analytic' will also be transcendental, since it is concerned with the application of the pure determining concepts to space (and time). But knowledge relating to materially filled determinate space, i.e. appearances, is not transcendental but empirical knowledge.

Grammatical. '*Der Gebrauch des Raumes von Gegenständen überhaupt*' ('the application of space to objects in general'— Kemp Smith): *through* or *by means of* objects; i.e. the application of objects in general *to* space.[5]

Fourth sentence [sixth sentence]. Cf. p. 81, 'Introductory'.

THIRD PARAGRAPH We thus expect that, in addition to the concepts derived from ('materially') organised nature and the concepts arising from the determinate forms of intuition, it will be possible to distinguish a new class of concepts designating those acts of thought, by means of which time and space are organised. It is with this new class of concepts that the science of transcendental logic is concerned.

The task of the new science will be to concern itself (1) with the origin of these concepts ('Metaphysical Deduction'), and (2) with the sphere of application and objective validity of these concepts ('Transcendental Deduction').

---

[5] By 'transcendental use of space' I understand its legitimate, not its illegitimate, use. It is scarcely to be expected that Kant should burden the explanation of his newly introduced concept of 'transcendental logic' by referring to 'transcendental misuse'. Moreover, objects are not things-in-themselves at all, but synthetic unities legitimately applied to space. 'Transcendental misuse' (A 296/B 353) is the application of the synthetic unity or category to a non-spatio-temporal, i.e. merely thought, intuition; cf. §§ 22 and 23.

The new science will have to be called logic, since the determination of space and time and thus the organisation of the whole of nature is based on actions of the understanding, i.e. logical actions. It will also have to be called transcendental because, whereas general logic is concerned with already formed concepts, the new science is concerned with the forms of intuition which have yet to be conceptually organised; i.e. it is concerned with the forming concept and thus with the ultimately formative sources of all phenomenal reality.

III THE DIVISION OF GENERAL LOGIC INTO ANALYTIC AND DIALECTIC

Introductory

In this and the following section Kant explains the significance of the critical distinction between analytic and dialectic.

The traditional analytic is pure general logic, i.e. traditional logic. The traditional dialectic is, according to Kant, traditional metaphysics, i.e. metaphysics which hopes to acquire knowledge by means of purely logical operations. Here Kant is particularly concerned to explain in what sense he can speak of the transcendental dialectic as a branch of traditional logic. Just as the transcendental analytic is concerned with the origin of those representations which correspond to phenomenal reality, so the transcendental dialectic is concerned with the origin of our metaphysical representations and speculations. Just as the transcendental analytic amounts to a critical investigation into the foundations of our knowledge of nature, so is the transcendental dialectic a critical investigation or rather refutation of all metaphysical (ontological) theories and systems.

In a certain respect Kant's 'Introduction' VI (B 19 to B 24), anticipates the content of the two sections considered here (A 57 to A 64, B 82 to B 88; cf. commentary to Kant's 'Introduction' VI).

Kant's discussion of the concept 'truth' and of the possibility of a 'universal criterion of truth' lends a special interest to the section here under discussion. In Kant's use of the term, 'truth' is subordinate to 'knowledge'. Truth is one of the three criteria of knowledge (§ 12, cf. below). That is, Kant uses the word 'truth' as a technical term signifying (1) agreement of a concept with its object, (2) consistency or agreement of a theory with itself. Neither of these two criteria of truth, says Kant, can be taken for universal criteria. Agreement with the object presupposes the observation and investigation of particulars and is thus not a unitary universal criterion; consistency or agreement with self, on the other hand, is a purely formal criterion, applicable to any system of thought whatever, irrespective of whether the system agrees with its object or not. It follows— and this is one of Kant's most important conclusions—that purely logical reflections are incapable by themselves of establishing truth, i.e. that traditional metaphysics is built on treacherous ground.

A certain irony is clearly detectable here in Kant's treatment of the concepts 'truth' and 'universal criterion of truth'. For truth in the full sense of the word is the ultimate goal not only of philosophers in particular but of people in general. The possession of such truth would mean the end of all our labours. Kant never uses the term 'truth' in this full sense. The whole truth is accessible only to the divine intellect, which presumably penetrates beyond the world of appearances to embrace things-in-themselves. But for us human beings only (limited) knowledge is possible. 'Knowledge' is defined by Kant as a verified hypothesis, i.e. a hypothesis which is (1) unitary, (2) confirmed by experience and consistent, (3) comprehensive, viz. applicable to all it is designed to cover (§ 12). Knowledge is thus achievable only with immense labour and care and with infinite observation of detail in each particular case. If it is so arduous to acquire knowledge, how foolish it is to seek a universal criterion of truth. To possess such a criterion would amount to knowledge of the very nature and structure of all things.

Résumé

Pure general logic, which is concerned solely with already formed concepts and already advanced theories, may be used only as an instrument of verification (canon) for the purpose of analysing the concepts and confirming or refuting the theories. If pure general logic is used as an instrument of construction (organon), it necessarily generates illusion and deception, for purely logical operations can produce no results outside already acquired knowledge.

There seems no need to explain in detail either this or the four following sections.

IV THE DIVISION OF TRANSCENDENTAL LOGIC INTO TRANSCENDENTAL ANALYTIC AND DIALECTIC

Résumé

However, pure general logic has been repeatedly used as an organon or instrument of construction, and indeed it has readily recommended itself for such purposes, the nature of man being what it is. As a result, such a constructive or synthetic use of pure logic becomes an object of transcendental philosophy. Unlike traditional philosophy, which constructs illusory metaphysical systems, transcendental philosophy makes it its task to investigate the misleading use of logic and the results to which such a constructive use of pure logic must inevitably lead.

Transcendental Analytic

ANALYTIC OF CONCEPTS

THE CLUE TO THE DISCOVERY OF ALL PURE CONCEPTS OF THE UNDERSTANDING

Introductory

Kant begins the 'Transcendental Analytic' with three short introductory sections. In the first he explains that, if the

TRANSCENDENTAL LOGIC

investigation of the 'Transcendental Analytic' is to reach its goal—viz. the deduction of the pure concepts of the understanding—it must be guided by four considerations: (1) the deduced concepts must be pure, i.e. formative and not derived from formed matter; (2) they must be concepts of the understanding, i.e. not concepts of unitary intuition (like simultaneity or extension) but concepts or rules of formative unitary thought; (3) they must be elementary concepts, not derivative concepts (cf. commentary to § 10); (4) the table of concepts must be complete. Kant adds that the fourth consideration necessitates an investigation based on the idea of a system as opposed to a haphazardly conducted enquiry.

In the second of these introductory sections Kant emphasises (as he does in the Preface to the first edition A XII) that his analysis is completely novel in character, since he is concerned not merely with analysing already formed familiar concepts but with investigating the formation of concepts by the understanding—or, to use his own words, with investigating the understanding itself.

Finally, in the third of these sections Kant repeats that any haphazardly conducted enquiry will be bound to fail; only an investigation based on the idea of a system will be able to lead to the desired result, namely, systematic completeness. Hence, just as the understanding must be construed as an 'absolute unity', so must all pure concepts of the understanding be described as a system of concepts, based on a single principle.

The principle which Kant has in mind here is the unitary point of view from which he describes any conceptual relation, namely *the relation of a higher order concept to the lower order concept which it implies* (cf. commentary to the following section).

Résumé

If the transcendental analytic is to realise its aim, viz. the deduction of all the conceptual elements contained in our knowledge of nature, it must be a systematic investigation, i.e. an investigation of the principle and basic rules of coherent thought.

Our aim is thus not to analyse concepts which are current and familiar but to inquire into the original source of all possible concepts.

Assuming that our faculty of understanding, i.e. the faculty of coherent thought, is a separate faculty quite different from sensibility and intuition, and in the expectation that it will be possible to describe coherent thought from one view point, we now make it our task systematically and exhaustively to describe the rules or forms of coherent thought in general.

THE LOGICAL EMPLOYMENT OF THE UNDERSTANDING

Introductory

The objection has been raised against Kant that he failed clearly to extricate his new synthetic logic from traditional logic; that his reform of logic was half-hearted and incomplete; that he arrived at absurd conclusions (cf. Kemp Smith's *Commentary*, p. 184). The extremely important section which we must now discuss and in which Kant, in order to construct the basis for his deduction of the categories, gives an account of his own concept of logic has been sharply criticised as totally inadequate (cf. Kemp Smith, loc. cit., p. 176).

KANT'S REFORM OF LOGIC II[6]

1. We have already said above that Kant's reform of logic consists essentially in this: whereas traditional logic, according to Kant, is a logic of Being—or, we can now add, of deduction and inference—Kant's logic is a logic of phenomenal reality and, generally speaking, construction.

We have also already suggested above how Kant was able to incorporate traditional logic into his own logical

[6] Cf. 'Kant's reform of logic' I, p. 20.

system. By reinterpreting traditional logic as a logic of already constructed reality and of already formed concepts, he distinguishes two logical modes: (1) the mode of constructive thought; (2) the mode of verificatory or clarificatory thought relating to already constructed reality or to the already formed concept. In supplementing his own new logic of construction with traditional logic, represented as a logic of already constructed reality, Kant brings the whole sphere of thought and experience under his system of united logic. The section here under discussion is based on the firm foundation of a complete, self-consistent, logical system.[7]

In other words; Kant is not here concerned with the distinction between synthetic and analytic judgements, nor with that between the two logical modes; he is concerned rather with judgements, and concepts in general, i.e. with logic in general, which embraces the two modes of constructive and clarificatory thought. For whether phenomenal reality is understood as already constructed or yet to be constructed, the picture or schema of Kant's logic of construction remains the same: it is basically different from the logic of deduction and inference.

2. The foundation of the distinction between traditional (ontological) and Kantian logic is as follows. The traditional view maintained that our various representations correspond to given reality—given, as it were, with their forms —and that they determine the relational structure of thought. The critical view maintains that the relational structure of thought determines the relation or mutual integration of our various representations. The traditional view implies that there may be many structural forms of thought: forms of the concept itself, e.g. Aristotle's categories, or forms by means of which concepts are related to each other. Kant, however, succeeds in bringing all coherent thought under one single principle: that of the higher order concept implying a lower order concept, i.e. as relation *within* the

[7] Cf. Paton, loc. cit., p. 256; also my paper 'The relation of transcendental and formal logic', in *Kant-Studien*, LI, pp. 349 ff.

concept. This is the *single* principle which Kant discusses in the introductory sections to the 'Metaphysical Deduction' (A 65/B 90): *the principle of synthetic unity applied to logic*.

The concept as synthetic unity or, more precisely, as synthetic unity within synthetic unity, which is the basic principle of Kant's logic, is a paradoxical assumption. The relation AB is conceived in two ways, $A > B$ and $A = B$, manifested in twelve forms or categories: as unity implying and being implied by multiplicity; as reality implying and being implied by limitation; as inherence implying and being implied by substance; as existence implying and being implied by possibility, etc.

The Kantian view of the yet-to-be-formed concept as synthetic unity amounts to this: the concept as synthetic unity is the representation of something which can be variously yet coherently described under each of its aspects. This representation can ultimately be described as the essence or form of the concept—essence and form being the same as the organised forms of intuition or, *in abstracto*, the category.

There is thus a basic difference between the traditional concept reflecting given reality and the Kantian concept imposing its form on phenomenal reality and capable of being filled with a variety of content. The traditional concept reflecting given reality connotes a given variety of properties or inherences, and denotes a given variety of objects. The Kantian concept, on the other hand, is the representation of a compound whole which can be variously yet coherently described by means of an indeterminate number of representations.

That is to say: the Kantian theory of the concept makes knowable nature into a unitary whole; its basic forms are fixed and it may be progressively explored in all its fullness in accordance with known and certain forms. This paradoxical view that the concept is a synthetic unity makes it possible to explain how knowledge of nature can be both *a priori* and *a posteriori*, or how nature can be spontaneously conceived and yet also known through objective experience. The universal form of synthetic unity in its twelve modes—which is nothing more than the organised forms of intuition or, *in abstracto*, the categories—introduces an element of necessity into all our knowledge; on the other hand, this form can be filled with an infinite variety of content.

3. Let us now turn to the important distinction between the traditional and the Kantian views of judgement. The traditional view is that the relation between concepts, a relation reflected or created by judgement, is independent of the concepts which the judgement links together. Kant, however, always construes the relation created by the judgement as the relation of a higher order concept to the lower order concept which it implies. That is to say, he maintains that *judgement reflects or is identical with the relational structure of the concept itself*. This, then, is Kant's important innovation. It is an innovation which enables him to derive the categories from a 'single principle'. The judgement, as understood by Kant, establishes such relation between concepts in twelve different modes. He construes these modes as necessary and, ultimately, as logical in character, i.e. as derived neither from experience of nature nor from the accidents of human psychology. Kant is thus able to develop the categories from a single root by maintaining, namely, that the relational structure of the concept itself is originally manifested in twelve different modes which precisely correspond to the modes of judgement.

The most important result of this theory is that the distinction between judgement and concept disappears and one basic logical form emerges. This achievement of Kant's has served as the starting point of all subsequent discussions of logical problems. It may be added that the Kantian concept (or synthetic representation) includes within itself not only judgement but also inference. The assumption of synthetic unity within synthetic unity or of the representation both implying and being implied by other representations involves an intermediate representation and signifies both triple and dual connection. However, Kant maintains that inference, or thought as mere logic, can lead only to arbitrary construction; knowledge can be reached only if the hierarchical relation of the higher order concept to the lower order concept is at the same time the relation of the determinate forms of spatio–temporal intuition to matter. That is to say: in order to establish knowledge the conceptual representation, variously yet coherently describable through its different aspects, must always refer to an entity of intuition, viz. a spatio–temporal object.

In contrast to traditional logic, which emphasises judgement and inference, Kant's logic is the logic of the concept. Concept is here understood both as actualised thought and as the act of coherent thought. His logic is thus a logic of construction. The traditional view of the act of thought is that it aims at defining, deducing or inferring something specific. According to Kant, the act of thought always construes what is indeterminate in the necessary form of the concept, i.e. of the category regarded as something variously describable or variously applicable.

Hence, the act of thought—or, to use Kant's own term, the function of the understanding—can always be described by means of the same schema, irrespective of whether the mode is analytic or synthetic and irrespective of whether the judgement is *a priori* or *a posteriori*: namely, as an act which imposes a necessary form on something which has yet to be determined by means of an intermediate element.

This makes Kant's logic, as distinct from the logic of deduction and inference, a logic of construction. One might even call it the logic of the scientific working hypothesis.

Thus, in reply to the critics of Kant who like Kemp Smith have complained about the inadequacy of Kant's reform of logic, we may say this: general logic is neither a disruptive element in, nor a superfluous accretion to, Kant's logic. On the contrary, general logic, as re-interpreted by Kant, fulfils a precisely defined function within Kantian logic: it both supplements and completes transcendental logic. We may also remark that Kant completed his work of logical reform in so far as he brought the whole sphere of thought and experience within his own system of transcendental logic with its supplement of traditional logic. Constructive and clarificatory (general) logic are only two sides or modes of Kantian logic. As a result, the whole realm of possible knowledge may be described in the modes of constructive and general logic. (On the limitations of Kant's logic cf. pp. 27 f., p. 138 and pp. 170 f.)

THE LOGICAL EMPLOYMENT OF THE UNDERSTANDING (*continued*)

Introductory (*continued*)

Kant's immediate intention in this section is chiefly to show that the forms of judgement are the rules of all coherent thought in general. Kant proves this by showing that judgement and concept are essentially the same, i.e. that both judgement and concept may be construed as conceptual relation or as relation *within* the concept.

Résumé

All coherent thought—according to the critical philosophy, spontaneously generated by the human mind—is conceptual in character. Conceptual representation, called knowledge when applied to something given, is always the representation of related representations. More precisely: a conceptual representation is nothing other than a higher order representation implying lower order representations.

The act of conceiving, taken in this sense, always corresponds to an act of judgement. Judgement can always be described as a higher order representation (concept or judgement) implying a lower order representation.

Now, there are certain ways, or forms, in which higher order representations can imply lower order representations; for example, the way in which unity implies multiplicity, the way in which substance implies inherence, or the way in which the ground implies the consequences.

Thus from the table of judgements we may deduce the forms of such conceptual relation, or relation within a concept; i.e. the forms of the judgement are the forms of coherent thought in general.

Explanation

As Kant has shown in the introductory section to the 'Transcendental Logic', knowledge always presupposes both intuition and conception. He is now in a position to discuss conception exhaustively.

Conception or coherent thought in general, Kant maintains, is spontaneous, i.e. it is originated not by the mind being affected by something but by the mind functioning in its own specific way, namely as the understanding. Kant defines the function[8] of the understanding or the act of thought, whether it be an act of conceiving or judging, as the act which determines what is indeterminate by means of a higher order representation implying lower order representations. That is to say: Kant maintains that mind, confronted with something indeterminate, comprehends it through its logical function as something variously yet coherently describable, or as various representations implied by a higher order representation.

Having thus defined coherent thought in general, Kant turns to the main point: the discussion of the judgement–concept relation. He looks at this relation from the standpoint of cognitive thought in general; i.e. from the viewpoint of coherent thought applied to something given.

The concept by itself does not constitute knowledge, says Kant. Only a concept embodied in a judgement can establish knowledge. He adds that ultimately the judgement must refer to intuition. In other words, he is maintaining that the human mind knows something given or a given

[8] On the meaning of the term 'function', cf. Paton's excellent philological exposition: Paton, loc. cit., pp. 245 ff.

TRANSCENDENTAL LOGIC

object of intuition by applying two different though combinable representations to it. The important point to notice here is this: such a double representation, applicable to something given, always has the form of a higher order concept implying a lower order concept.

Judgement can be defined, then, as the 'mediate knowledge of an object' or as 'the representation of a representation of an object', i.e. judgement is described as conceptual relation applicable to something given. This definition implicitly expresses the basic critical idea that all human knowledge is indirect. There is only one kind of direct relation to an object, and that is intuition; but our intuition is not the same as knowledge. Thus only an intuitive intellect, i.e. an intellect not divided into the two faculties of conception and intuition, can possess immediate knowledge, namely by intellectual intuition or intuitive conception.

At this point Kant interrupts the account of his proof in order to illustrate by means of an example what has been said so far. (The passage extends from the words 'In every judgement' to 'is collected into one'.)

The higher order concept in the judgement 'all bodies are divisible' is the concept 'divisible'; it implies, *inter alia*, the concept 'body', which is applicable to certain objects of intuition. Similarly, the relation 'body : divisible' may be applied to those objects. We may, hence, say that we know a number of objects by means of the judgement 'all bodies are divisible'; or that the human mind indirectly represents a number of objects, namely 'bodies', by means of the higher order concept 'divisible'.

Kant now sums up the argument he has just illustrated with the remark that all knowledge or all cognitive thought can be described as judgement, i.e. as a higher order concept implying a lower order concept.

Having thus shown that every judgement can be represented as concept, he goes on in the final part of his proof to argue that every concept can be described as judgement.

When, says Kant, we grasp something given by means of

judgement and concept, or when we apply two different but related representations to something given, we use the representations inherent in it to describe this something as unitary. This doctrine represents the logical side of the main critical conclusion that the spatio-temporal object constructed by the human mind, although it may have infinite content, is, however, necessarily bound to a specific form.

This last part of Kant's argument may also be explained as follows. Having discussed the concept from the connotative point of view in the example 'body : divisible', he now examines it from the denotative point of view ('body : metal'). He shows that in both cases the relation inherent in the corresponding judgement is the same as the relation of the higher order concept to the lower order concept which it implies. The human understanding, Kant maintains, when it is confronted with the indeterminate, grasps it not only as something which can be described in various ways but also as something which can be variously applied, i.e. as a concept which not only connotes the representations it contains within it but also denotes the objects it embraces. In Kant's example, body, as the lower order concept, connotes 'divisibility'; as the higher order concept it denotes 'metal'. Now, according to the critical philosophy, a concept which is applicable to phenomenal reality is a concept realised in space and time. A concept denoting a number of objects is the determinate forms of intuition capable of being filled with a variety of content. In other words: the various concepts implied connotatively or denotatively in an empirical concept all depend on one conceptual form (that of the higher order concept implying a lower order concept). It is by means of this single conceptual form that the indeterminate is rendered determinate.

Finally, it follows that the judgement can always be described as relation within a concept and that the forms of judgements are the same as the forms of coherent thought in general.

SECTION 9

Introductory

To prepare the reader for his new table of categories, Kant presents in § 9 a table of judgements which is basically the traditional logical schema. The two sections, §§ 9 and 10, must be taken as a whole. Kant's intention here is to show that certain rules of thought contained in the table of judgements can be understood, not only as the rules for judging already formed phenomenal reality, but also as the rules regulating the original formation of phenomenal reality in general; i.e. as the rules underlying all our conceptual and intuitive representations of phenomenal reality.

The 'Metaphysical Deduction' may be explained briefly as follows: Kant succeeds in showing that it is possible *to interpret certain rules of thought, discoverable in the table of judgements, as rules of the synthetic determination of time.* For example, he shows that the rule contained in the judgement $S = P$ (first moment of 'relation') is the conceptual principle of substance. Kant further shows that this principle is the same as a norm of time-determination—the norm, namely, of the enduring representation into which another representation is integrated as co-enduring and simultaneous.[9]

In this way, Kant shows that the rules of coherent thought discoverable in the table of judgements can be described as

---

[9] That is, according to Kant's theory the paradoxical concept of the synthetic whole, representable as unity through diverse representations, is intelligible only in its reference to time. This paradoxical representation is generated by our own mind, reacting on the one hand to the given matter by means of various sensations and capable, on the other hand, of representing or intuiting unity—the kind of unity capable of embracing an infinite number of diverse representations. Such represented or intuited unity is the spontaneously generated representation of a *single* time. The human mind, capable of receiving diverse representations, generates the concept of substance by thinking the whole, uniformly composed of diverse representations; it generates the intuition of substance by intuiting uniform time, composed of such simultaneous representations (cf. also pp. 195 ff.).

the formative principles of all synthetic unity, both intuited and conceived. For it emerges that the rules contained in the judgement and applied to primary content, viz. time and space, may be described as the conceptual archetypes (categories) of both empirical concepts and empirical intuitions, and hence of phenomenal reality in general.

A contradiction has been detected between Kant's assertion at the beginning of § 9 (that the judgement must be regarded from a purely formal point of view) and his explanation at the beginning of the second explanatory note (that content is not without a certain significance for transcendental logic).

But what he obviously means is this: in order to discover the purely formal rules of coherent thought in the table of judgements, the content must be ignored; in order to discover the rules of constructive or formative thought, i.e. the categories, the content must be taken into account. That is to say: whereas judgement by itself, as pure logic, must be examined from a purely formal point of view, content is important for discovering the categories which depend on metaphysics and logic combined. What Kant says here is perfectly consistent with one of his most important conclusions, namely that pure formal logic establishes no knowledge, while transcendental logic, or rather the category (applied to primary intuition), is not only the basis of all our knowledge but also the very foundation of phenomenal reality in general. Cf. also the commentary to the last paragraph of § 14.

Kant has frequently been criticised both for his dependence on traditional logic and for the way in which he works out his scheme of categories in detail. Of course, his doctrine of the necessity of the categories is unprovable; Kant himself hinted that he regarded them as axiomatic (cf. § 21). But he did share the conviction of his contemporaries that the rules of traditional logic are immutable and absolutely necessary; he also believed that there could be no more secure foundation for his own system than traditional logic. Indeed—and there can be no doubt about this—Kant himself regarded the fact that he had succeeded in equating the logical forms of judgement with the norms of time-determination as the decisive proof of the truth of his own revolutionary philosophy.

Résumé

By regarding judgement, in which all (coherent) thought must be expressed, from a purely formal point of view, we can exhaustively describe the forms or rules of coherent thought under four titles, each of which contains three moments.

Explanation

The table of judgements

I *Quantity*
  1. P is asserted of all S: general judgement. (All men are mortal.)
  2. P is asserted of some S: particular judgement. (Some men die young.)
  3. P is asserted of one S: singular judgement. (Caius is mortal.)

II *Quality*
  1. S is P: affirmative. (The soul is immortal.)
  2. S is not P: negative. (The soul is not immortal.)
  3. S is not-P: infinite. (The soul is not-mortal.)

III *Relation*
  1. P is asserted of S without limitation: categorical. (The government of the world is perfectly just.)
  2. The equation of S and P depends on the equation of S' and P': hypothetical. (If the government of the world were perfectly just the wicked would always be punished.)
  3. S equals either P or P' or P'': disjunctive. (The world has arisen either through blind chance or through inner necessity or through an external cause.)

IV. *Modality*
  1. The equation of S and P is possible: problematic. (If the

government of the world were perfectly just—i.e. the government of the world either is or is not perfectly just.)
2. The equation of S and P is actual: assertoric. (Since the government of the world is to be regarded as perfectly just, the wicked will be punished—i.e. the punishment of the wicked is regarded as actual on the basis of the foregoing assumption.)
3. The equation of S and P is necessary: apodeictic. (Since the government of the world is perfectly just, the wicked will necessarily be punished—i.e. the concept (judgement) of the just government of the world necessarily involves the concept (judgement) of the punishment of the wicked.)

Kant's table of judgements—which must, of course, be studied in conjunction with his table of categories (cf. below)—differs in certain respects from the table of judgements current at the time (cf. Kemp Smith, loc. cit., pp. 192 ff.). In particular, Kant has introduced a trichotomy in place of a dichotomy in the first two sections, quantity and quality. He adds four explanatory paragraphs, each of which refers to one division of judgements: the first two are intended to explain his deviation from the usual dichotomous schema; the last two are of a generally explanatory nature.

The reason why Kant introduced a trichotomy instead of the usual dichotomy is briefly as follows. In general logic the relation S–P is treated as determinate; in transcendental logic it must be regarded as a relation which has yet, in certain respects of a formal nature, to be determined. That is to say: the judgement must be investigated, not merely as a means of expressing a relation between determinate S and determinate P, but as a means of formally determining S–P in certain respects.

EXPLANATORY NOTE 1 If P is universal (e.g. 'mortal') and S (as in traditional logic) is determinate (the concept 'all men' as embracing 'Caius'), it is a matter of indifference whether P is asserted of the universal S ('all men') or of the individual *S* ('Caius'). That is, since *S* as a formed concept can be equated with both the individual and the universal *S*, there is no need to distinguish between universal and singular judgements.

If, on the other hand, *S* is regarded as indeterminate—i.e. as a concept which has yet to be formed—the form of the judgement, which is either universal or singular, can be said to be quantitatively determinative. For if *P* is asserted of *S* in the logical form of a universal judgement, *S* is determined as 'all': totality. If *P* is asserted of *S* in the logical form of a singular judgement, *S* is determined as one: unity. Hence, in the transcendental logic—with reference to the deduction of the categories—the distinction between general and singular judgements is of importance.[10]

[10] Unfortunately, when writing this commentary I was not directly acquainted with Magdalena Aebi's critical work on Kant (*Kants Begründung der 'Deutschen Philosophie'*, Basel, 1947). The work attacks Kant's treatment of judgement. The book came to my notice through Heinrich Scholz's review in the *Deutsche Literaturzeitung* (vol. LXX, Nos. 8 and 9, pp. 342 ff.) and Georg Siegmund's paper 'Die Ueberwindung des Kantianismus' in the *Philosophisches Jahrbuch* (vol. LX, Nos. 2 and 3, pp. 267 f.). According to M. Aebi (cf. G. Siegmund, loc. cit., p. 271), if this aspect of Kant's theory were to agree with his philosophy as a whole, the judgements of quantity should have been distinguished from each other by subsuming a subject-concept under a predicate in three different ways. In fact, however, these judgements differ from each other according to the subject-concept. ('All men are mortal' contains a general subject; 'Caius is mortal' a singular subject.) Now, it is doubtless true that these judgements, traditionally viewed, i.e. construed as assertions connecting a given *S* with a given *P*, differ from each other according to the subject. But what particularly distinguishes transcendental logic is the view that a judgement is not an assertion *S–P* but a function which first establishes the relation *S–P*. If the judgement is looked at from the point of view of 'quantity', a relation of quantity is indeed established; but this relation, construed as pure concept of the understanding, is the category of quantity with its three moments upon which all *given* subject-concepts depend. That is to say: Kant's view is that judgements (of quantity) differ from each other primarily, not according to the subject-concepts, nor according to the different kinds of subsumption, but basically through a triple function manifesting itself in the judgements—a function through which

EXPLANATORY NOTE 2 If the relation S–P is regarded as determinate with respect to reality (the reality or non-reality of the mortal soul) then the two judgements 'the soul is immortal' and 'the soul is non-mortal' mean the same thing. That is to say: since the concept 'non-mortal' includes the concept 'immortal', both judgements affirm the reality of the non-mortal soul.

If, on the other hand, S–P is regarded as indeterminate with respect to reality, i.e. if the soul—immortal or non-mortal—is construed as a concept which has yet to be formed, we can say of the judgement that through its form it has an (implicitly) formative effect; for while the affirmative judgement 'the soul is immortal' affirms the reality of the immortal soul, the infinite judgement 'the soul is non-mortal' limits the affirmation to the reality or existence of the soul (in contrast to the mortal body), i.e. it affirms the substance of the 'soul' without actually affirming any particular property of the concept.

EXPLANATORY NOTE 3 Under the third title ('relation') Kant, rather than converting a dichotomy into a trichotomy, converts a somewhat cumbersome schema into a simpler threefold schema (cf. Kemp Smith, pp. 192 f.). Kant is particularly concerned here with the distinction he proposes to make between the category of causality and that of community. While the former corresponds to the logical relation between what conditions and what is conditioned, the category of community is suggested by the 'community of mutually exclusive cognitions'; i.e. Kant distinguishes a class of judgements where one of a certain limited number of possible predicates is necessarily asserted of the subject.

---

something indeterminate is rendered determinate by means of the relation of two representations to each other. (For example, *triangle* : *equilateral*, where triangle is a part of what is implicit in equilateral; particular judgement.) This function, which may also be construed as our faculty of universal, particular or singular representations in general, is what first makes possible the universal particular or singular subject-concepts which appear in judgements construed as *assertions*.

TRANSCENDENTAL LOGIC

EXPLANATORY NOTE 4 There is a certain unmistakable similarity between this note and § 11 (added in the second edition), where Kant speaks of 'some nice points suggested by the table of categories'. Kant here compares the three moments of modality—the problematic, the assertoric and the apodeictic—with the three faculties: understanding, judgement and reason. For understanding, the content of knowledge is indeterminate but determinable ('problematic'); for judgement it is determinate and expressible ('assertoric'); for reason it is necessarily as it is, i.e. inferable (apodeictic). Or: the understanding is the faculty of determining; judgement is the faculty of expressing what is determinate; reason is the faculty of inferring what is necessarily as it is. Kant adds: the first moment of modality also corresponds to formulating a hypothesis; the second to asserting that the hypothesis is right; the third to concluding that the hypothesis is necessarily correct.

SECTION 10

Introductory

The present section completes the metaphysical deduction (cf. the commentary, 'Introductory' to § 9, on the purpose and significance of the metaphysical deduction). This is an important section and, apart from the 'Transcendental Deduction', more illuminating than any other single section of the *Critique of Pure Reason*. Kant here introduces the concepts of 'synthesis', 'pure synthesis', 'intuition in general' and 'the manifold of intuition in general'; he also characterises space and time as media. He explains that analysis is a secondary act of thought, whereas synthesis is an original act of thought—i.e. it is here that Kant develops his doctrine of validly constructive thought.

The following is a brief account of the first part of § 10. Synthesis (the act of coherent thought) is the act by means of which we unify various representations; pure synthesis is synthesis which refers to pure elements. Synthesis in general is the operation of the imagination, i.e. our faculty of joining a given manifold together. Synthesis of the understanding (the synthesis with which Kant is here concerned) is described as logical (conceptual) synthesis. Pure conceptual synthesis, applied to pure elements (e.g. space and time), produces the category (the rules of coherent constructive thought realised in space and time *are* the categories). The categorical representation of an object is its objective representation, i.e. knowledge of that object. Finally, the act of judgement (as coherent thought) turns out to be essentially the same as the act which constructs phenomenal reality by means of the forms of spatio–temporal intuition.

Résumé

FIRST PARAGRAPH In whatever way we may describe thought, it must always refer to something. However, our concept of validly constructive thought requires the assumption of a special something to which such thought refers; it requires the assumption, namely, of media (space and time). These media are indeterminately given, but once they are determined they themselves exercise a determinative function. We now introduce the term 'synthesis', which signifies validly constructive thought referring to such pure or materially filled media.

SECOND PARAGRAPH Validly constructive thought referring merely to the pure media is called pure synthesis.

THIRD PARAGRAPH We differentiate between the merely psychological faculty of combining various representations, i.e. the faculty of imagination, and the faculty of understanding called synthesis and referring to the mediating forms of intuition or mediated nature. We say that our logical faculty makes possible, not merely connection, but also unification. That is to say, our logical faculty imposes its law on the confused faculty of imagination.

FOURTH PARAGRAPH The categories are generated by the

TRANSCENDENTAL LOGIC

operation of pure logical synthesis on a pure medium like space and time.

FIFTH PARAGRAPH Thus the task of transcendental philosophy is to interpret determinate space and time conceptually, i.e. categorically. It will then be possible to explain how knowledge, which presupposes both indeterminately given elements and the connective faculty of imagination, ultimately depends on our logical faculty, i.e. the faculty of uniting what is diverse in a determinate and necessary manner (namely, according to the category).

SIXTH PARAGRAPH It can now be seen not only that judgement is essentially the same as concept, but also that the act of judgement is an act of unification, in the same sense as the original act of transforming what is indeterminate into (synthetic) unity is also an act of unification. For in judgement we unite different representations, concepts or judgements; but our original act is an act which transforms mere succession into duration, simultaneity and ordered succession. From the forms of judgement it is hence possible to deduce the forms of time-determination, understood as the original forms of validly constructive thought, i.e. as categories.

Explanation

FIRST PARAGRAPH *First sentence*. The content of general logic comes from sources outside itself, i.e. its content consists of compound representations, empirical or pure, which must be explained—of synthetic representations, which must be analysed.

Second sentence [*second and third sentences*]. Transcendental logic, on the other hand, refers to a special content, namely an intuitable manifold. Without this manifold its concepts would be 'empty', i.e. neither realisable nor describable.

Third sentence [*fourth sentence*]. For us[11] that special content (or primary matter) is a manifold which is given as a

[11] Cf. commentary of §§ 21 and 23.

succession of representations which refer to three-dimensional form; i.e. it is the indeterminate forms of intuition. These forms are also the conditions which hold for every thing which affects us or which we (spontaneously) represent, and which therefore have an influence on even our conceptual representations of objects.

It is in this highly illuminating sentence that Kant clearly characterises space and time as media.[12]

Grammatical. die mithin auch den Begriff derselben jederzeit affizieren müssen ('which therefore must also always affect the concept of these objects'). *die* ('which') refers to conditions; *derselben* ('of the same') means 'of those objects'.

Fourth sentence [*fifth sentence*]. If we regard the thinking mind as alone spontaneous we assume that it transforms the given manifold into synthetic unity, or that it grasps spatio–temporal phenomena by taking their individual moments, examining them, fixing them in the memory and finally uniting them together. In this way it creates the object, known or to be known. That is: coherent thought, applied to what is given, is validly constructive.

Fifth sentence [*sixth sentence*]. Such an act of thought is called synthesis.

SECOND PARAGRAPH *First sentence*. Synthesis in general, both pure and empirical, is an act which unites various representations and thus creates the knowable object.

Kant here defines coherent thought, or thought in general, as a unity composed of different representations.

Second sentence. Pure synthesis is an act which unites a pure manifold, e.g. the manifold given to us as a succession of representations which refers to three dimensional form.

Kant defines pure thought as a pure united manifold, or as thought manifesting itself in a determinable and universally applicable element, e.g. space–time.

Third sentence. All analytic thought refers to representa-

[12] Kant expresses himself still more clearly on the medial character of space and time in the chapter 'Schematism'; A 138 f./B 177 f.

tions compoundly given, i.e. to synthetic (conceptual) representations. No concept, i.e. no representation referring to already constructed reality or to determinate pure intuition, can be the result of analysis. On the contrary, any analysable concept depends on antecedent construction. On the other hand, certain conceptual forms (e.g. the so-called 'predicables'; cf. below, p. 115 f.) can be arrived at by logical analysis.

This sentence expresses one of Kant's most important ideas, the idea that logical synthesis is the substance of all phenomenal reality, or, more generally, that logical synthesis is the substance of everything intuitable (cf. 'Transcendental Deduction').

Fourth sentence [*fourth, fifth, sixth and seventh sentences*]. Even if the products of synthetic thought (empirical or pure) are unclear and confused and require clarification by analysis, none the less all analysis must necessarily be preceded by synthesis, the original act of cognitive thought.

THIRD PARAGRAPH *First sentence*. Synthesis in general—i.e. synthesis by itself, or mere synthesis—can be defined as the connective faculty in general, i.e. as imagination.

Kant here, as in the first edition of the 'Deduction' (to which he alludes) discusses the functions of imagination and memory (cf. the first paragraph). In the second edition of the 'Deduction', however, Kant has already to a certain extent distanced himself from the psychological theories current at the time (and also from the influence of Hume). Admittedly, he still agrees with the then generally prevalent psychological theory of imagination according to which (1) all our acts of connection are acts of imagination and (2) our imagination cannot do more than connect given representations. However, Kant, at this later period of his development, presupposes the theory of the mere synthesis of imagination and thinks it superfluous to mention it within the framework of his new theory.

Second sentence. But what transforms the given manifold

into knowable (synthetic) unity is not mere synthesis but conceptual synthesis or synthesis of the understanding.

That is to say: it is conceptual synthesis and not merely connective imagination which produces, for example, the 'picture' of a house from various representations. Connective imagination by itself cannot produce a determinate spatial form from various sensations; it can only produce subjective representations and fluctuating lines.

FOURTH PARAGRAPH *First sentence*. Pure synthesis, i.e. validly constructive thought in general, applied to a pure given manifold, is the pure concept of the understanding.

That is: the category is to be construed as the fourfold form, in which the manifold can be originally transformed into synthetic unity.

Second sentence [*second and third sentences*]. Pure synthesis, i.e. any act of pure thought, is based on a form or type of synthetic unity (original or derivative); e.g. counting is an act of pure synthesis based on the pure concept of the decade (cf. commentary to Kant's 'Introduction' V). Kant says here that pure synthesis, which is what concerns him, is conceptual synthesis, i.e. an act by means of which any given manifold is logically unified. The decade is, in Kant's terminology, one of the predicables or a derivative pure concept of the understanding under the category of quantity.

Third sentence [*fourth sentence*]. Because such synthesis is conceptual in character, whatever it generates is necessarily as it is. This sentence is based on the doctrine of validly constructive thought, i.e. thought which forms both phenomenal reality and pure intuition. Kant maintains: if there were no universal necessary rules or norms regulating the transformation of the manifold into synthetic unity, we should be unable to construct necessary, i.e. objective, representations (and consequently acquire knowledge) from our various sensations; we should have only accidental, fluctuating representations.

FIFTH PARAGRAPH *First sentence*. General logic is concerned

TRANSCENDENTAL LOGIC

with compound representations; it clarifies them conceptually and unifies them.

Second sentence. Transcendental logic is concerned with the pure manifold. It unifies it conceptually. That is to say: transcendental logic shows how synthetic unity can be represented logically (conceptually) as the quadruply manifested form of the unified manifold, i.e. as categories.

Third sentence [*third and fourth sentences*]. If we wish to describe the pure concepts, the first element (or primary matter) we must assume as given is the pure manifold; second, we must assume a spontaneous faculty—imagination—inherent in ourselves: this faculty is a faculty of connecting anything which may be given. However, such an act of imagination cannot establish knowledge.

Fourth sentence [*fifth sentence*]. Our *understanding* thus transforms the given manifold into a knowable object by means of certain norms or rules of unification—rules which are simply the forms of synthetic unity, or forms without which there could be no synthetic unity.

In this fifth paragraph Kant once more sums up the argument of the previous sections in preparation for the conclusions of the crucial sixth paragraph.

SIXTH PARAGRAPH *Introductory*. Kant is now in a position to show that the categories can be deduced from the forms of judgement.

What is the category? It is coherent thought in general, construed as constructive thought. What are the categories? They are types of coherent thought in general, viewed as constructive thought. What is coherent thought, or, to use Kant's own words, the function of the understanding in general? It is the act by means of which different representations are united. Now, such an act of uniting diverse representations can be expressed by means of the traditional judgement. As a result, all types of coherent thought must be discoverable in the traditional judgement. The traditional judgement refers to constructed reality. Hence, we can describe the types of coherent constructive thought, if we construe the rules applying to judgement, not as rules of thought referring to constructed reality, but as rules of thought referring to some pure manifold.

But this cannot be done *in abstracto*. It can be done only if the rules applying to the judgement, i.e. to constructed reality, are understood as manifested in a given manifold, namely space and time.

Thus if the forms of judgement are reinterpreted as the forms of original synthetic time-determination, the categories can be deduced; i.e. the types of constructive thought can be found and described.

First sentence. The very faculty which unites diverse representations referring to already constructed reality or intuition by means of judgement also unifies the pure manifold into synthetic unity. Such synthetic unity is conceptual in nature and can therefore be called a pure concept of the understanding.

'Mere synthesis': synthesis of the imagination.

Second sentence [*second and third sentences*]. The understanding judges on the basis of determinate space and time (i.e. by means of analytic unity); the same understanding generates the concept of the object in general, by determining space and time (i.e. by transforming the manifold into synthetic unity).

Here follows a still more precise paraphrase of this difficult sentence.

The understanding judges, i.e. unites various representations referring to already constructed reality or to intuition by means of analytic unity. *Analytic unity* is the unity of the materially filled and logically organised forms of intuition; these latter, understood as concept, imply their own moments. Hence the understanding, by judging, unites diverse representations on the basis of certain forms inherent in the conceptual representation, i.e. on the basis of determinate space and time.

By means of a corresponding original act of unification—

an act which unites the pure manifold, e.g. space and time—the understanding introduces 'transcendental content' (determinate time) into its own pure representations. For this reason the representations peculiar to the understanding can be regarded as pure, object-forming concepts of the understanding. This is a class of concepts unknown to general logic.

SEVENTH PARAGRAPH A table of categories can thus be drawn up which corresponds, title for title and moment for moment, to the table of judgements.

Table of categories

I *Quantity*
1. The indeterminate is conceived as unity. The manifold of representations, given as succession, is transformed into the representation of a single enduring time.
2. The indeterminate is conceived as plurality. The manifold of representations, given as succession, is transformed into the representation of parts of time succeeding each other in a determinate order.
3. The indeterminate is conceived as totality. The manifold of representations, given as succession, is transformed into the representation of an enduring time composed of parts succeeding each other.

Note. It can be seen why Kant deduced the category of unity from the general judgement and the category of totality from the singular judgement—a deduction which has occasioned surprise and been much criticised as 'highly artificial' (cf. Kemp Smith, loc. cit., p. 196). The judgement 'all men are mortal', which unites 'all men' under the concept 'mortal', establishes conceptual unity. The judgement 'Caius is mortal', in which 'mortal' refers to all the representations implicit in the representation of the individual Caius, establishes conceptual totality and thus indicates the category of totality.

II *Quality*
1. Unity is understood as actualised: reality. (Determinate) time is conceived as materially filled time.

2. Unity is understood as not actualised: negation. Time is conceived as empty.
3. Unity is understood as still to be actualised: limitation. Time (to-be-determined) is conceived as partially filled.

III *Relation*
1. The indeterminate is determined (conceived) as substance with its inherences. The manifold of representations, given as succession, is transformed into the representation of enduring time composed of simultaneous parts.
2. The indeterminate is determined (conceived) as states of substance, of which each determines its successor: cause and effect. The manifold of representations, given as succession, is transformed into the representation of parts of time, of which one necessarily precedes the other.
3. The indeterminate is determined (conceived) as states of substance mutually determining each other: community. The manifold of representations, given as succession, is transformed into the representation of parts of time, which, within one time, are necessarily simultaneous with each other.

IV *Modality*
1. The indeterminate is understood as determinable/non-determinable: possibility–impossibility. The manifold of representations, given as succession, is transformable/non-transformable into determinate time (and determinate space).
2. The indeterminate is understood as determinate/non-determinate: existence–non-existence. The manifold of representations given as succession, is transformed/not-transformed into determinate time (and determinate space).
3. The indeterminate is understood as determining/non-determining: necessity–contingency. The manifold of representations, given as succession, is transformed/not-transformed into determining time (and determining space).

The remaining paragraphs of § 10 do not seem to require any detailed explanation. The first of these paragraphs contains a criticism of the Aristotelian categories which Kant describes as being merely 'patched together', unlike his own categories which he describes as being based on a *single* principle. It is true, as we have already shown, that Kant's categories taken as a whole are simply the twelve possible

TRANSCENDENTAL LOGIC

types of a basic conceptual relation—the relation, namely, of a higher order concept to a lower order concept which it implies.

For the explanation of the two following paragraphs, see Kant's 'Introduction' VII, which contains his first mention of the pure, derivative concepts of the understanding, the predicables. Kant says in this section of his 'Introduction' that in a system of pure reason it would be necessary to give an exhaustive account of the predicables, but that in a critique of pure reason such an exhaustive account is not necessary. In the present section under discussion Kant is somewhat more detailed; he gives some examples of predicables and outlines their derivation. Thus, for Kant, 'force', 'action' and 'passion' are concepts derived from the concept of causality, or from the concept of matter operating on matter in accordance with causal laws. On the other hand, the concepts of 'coming into being' and 'passing away' are contained in the representations (for the human understanding[13]) of matter assuming or losing determinability, i.e. they can be regarded as derived from the category of modality.

Finally, in the last paragraph of § 10, Kant raises the question whether the categories can be defined. He answers in the affirmative but declines to offer the definitions. Kant's position here (apparently) contradicts the discussion to be found in the first but not the second edition of the chapter 'Phenomena and Noumena' (A 241; A 244 f.). Kant there says (A 241), 'We realise that we are unable to define them (the categories) even if we wished'—'without, as he later adds (A 245), 'perpetrating a circle'. But it would be possible to define the categories 'schematically' (A 245).

Kant obviously felt that, for example, a definition of the category of quantity (first moment) as multiplicity determined as unity, or of the category of quality (first moment) as unity generated from multiplicity, etc.—that such merely

[13] Whereas for the divine intellect there is neither 'coming to be' nor 'passing away'.

formal definitions would be tautological and uninformative (cf. also the commentary to the chapter 'Phenomena and Noumena' on this apparent contradiction; cf. p. 212 f.).

SECTIONS 11 AND 12

Introductory

The two sections, §§ 11 and 12, first make their appearance in the second edition. Their chief purpose is, doubtless, to meet certain objections raised against Kant's table of categories (cf. in this connection Kemp Smith, loc. cit., pp. 198 ff.). In § 11 Kant wishes to prove that all the concepts he has characterised as categories are in fact ultimate or primary concepts. In § 12 he tries to show that certain other *a priori* concepts, derived from the schoolmen, are not to be added to the table of categories but are already implicit in Kant's own table of categories.

SECTION 11

Résumé

Some not unimportant remarks may be added in connection with the table of categories:

1. The categories may be divided into two main groups: (1) the mathematical and (2) the dynamical categories. That is: coherent thought may be understood as (1) unity of conceiving and (2) as consistency of argument.
2. Although it is true that, in the case of all four titles, the third category in each case is the product of the other two categories combined, none the less the third category always contains a conceptual moment absent from the other two; the third category is thus always ultimate and primary.
3. The category of community in fact corresponds to the disjunctive judgement in the following sense: community of objects means the mutual relation of (co-existent) parts within one (enduring, i.e. identical)

whole; similarly, in a disjunctive judgement the concepts referring to the parts stand in a mutually exclusive relation to each other within the sphere of the concept which embraces (and affirms) all these parts.

Explanation

KANT'S FIRST NOTE The distinction between two basic groups of categories corresponds to the distinction between nature as an object (of intuition) and nature as energy or active force; or between nature as something enduring and identical and nature as something coming into being and passing away. We may thus say that the categories of the first group arise from the transformation of the manifold into logical unity, i.e. concept, while the categories of the second group arise from the transformation of the manifold into logical movement or relation, i.e. judgement and inference.

It follows that the category corresponding to objective nature can be distinguished from the category corresponding to active changing nature. That is, coherent thought can be construed in two senses: (1) as unitary thought and (2) as consistent thought.

KANT'S SECOND NOTE The objection was raised that Kant's trichotomy of categories (within each of the four titles) was in fact only a dichotomy, since in each case a third but secondary concept is illegitimately introduced as a category. Kant's reply consists in pointing out that in each case the third category contains a moment not present in the other two categories. For example, the moment of finitude is contained in the concept of 'number' but is absent from the two categories of 'multiplicity' and 'unity' (embracing infinity) which combined produce 'totality'.

KANT'S THIRD NOTE Finally, Kant regards it as necessary to explain and defend the derivation of the category of community from the disjunctive judgement (cf. résumé and also the commentary to the table of judgements).

It is easy to see that the just discussed § 11, particularly Kant's first note (with the there introduced concept of the dynamic category) and the second note (which so strongly emphasises the importance of the trichotomy), contain important starting points for the Hegelian dialectic.

SECTION 12

Résumé

The famous scholastic axiom *quodlibet ens est unum verum bonum* can be given a critical interpretation. The axiom can be construed as synonymous with the category of quantity and its three moments. This can be done by making the axiom refer, not to already constructed objects, but to cognitive and creative thought in general. The axiom, reinterpreted in this sense, contains a sufficient criterion of what a correct or successful hypothesis is, i.e. a sufficient criterion of thought, applicable to reality and synonymous with knowledge.

Explanation

An axiom as old and as frequently quoted as this one must, says Kant, have a certain value and possess at least a grain of truth. Of course, it is necessary to understand it correctly. *Unum* must be interpreted as the unity of the concept; *verum* as the multiple applications of such a concept to reality; *bonum* as the completeness or totality of such applications, i.e. their exclusive and perfect agreement with that concept. In this way, Kant equates the triple principle of *unum verum bonum* with the category of quantity in its three moments, and construes it as a triple criterion of possible knowledge.

Textual (B 115). I regard *verwandeln* ('transform') as corrupt and suggest it be replaced by *verwenden* ('employ' or 'apply'). *Verwandeln*—apart from rhetorical or poetical language—needs to be completed by the phrase *in etwas* ('into something'). In any case, the word *nur* ('only') aptly qualifies *verwenden*: the logical criteria of possibility are *only* (*nur*) generally applied to the quality of a cognition; it is not possible with *verwandeln*.

We now come to the last and most interesting part of § 12, where Kant explains his concept of 'truth'. According to Kant, 'truth', in the sense of truth accessible to man, is synonymous with a correct or successful hypothesis, i.e. with knowledge (cf. pp. 86 ff. above).

An acceptable hypothesis, says Kant, must be (1) unitary, (2) consistent and applicable to the reality to which it refers, (3) sufficient and comprehensive.

We may here add that Kant's system itself is an example of a successfully executed hypothesis: it is unitary; it is consistent and applicable to experience; it is sufficient to explain that experience and it is all-embracing.

KANT'S TRANSITION TO THE TRANSCENDENTAL DEDUCTION OF THE CATEGORIES

SECTIONS 13 AND 14

Introductory

The section of the *Critique of Pure Reason* consisting of §§ 13 and 14 is, it seems to me, often read with particular attention and frequently made the basis of an explanation of the critical philosophy in general. Kant himself refers to this part of the book in the first edition of the Preface (A XVII). He emphasises that the objective deduction is of greater importance than the subjective deduction and adds that what he says in this connection on pages 92 and 93 'should in any case [*allenfalls*] suffice by itself'. And yet this section is only Kant's introduction to the 'Transcendental Deduction of the Categories'. In § 13 he does no more than pose his problem; in § 14 he briefly offers a solution to the problem and hints at the way in which the proof will have to be carried out.

Both §§ 13 and 14 contain passages which have been misunderstood and misinterpreted and which have occasioned the criticisms that the argument is both inconsistent and circular. Kant's account of his *problem* has been taken for an account of his *theory*; this has led to the accusation of inconsistency. His discussion of the way in which the coming proof will be carried out has been taken from context and construed as ambiguous and capable of being applied in two ways; this has given rise to the criticism that Kant committed the vicious circle fallacy. See below, pp. 122 f. and 125 ff.

KANT'S TRANSITION

SECTION 13

Introductory

The purpose of the metaphysical deduction was to derive the categories as the determinative norms of thought. The task of the transcendental deduction is to explain how the categories can be determinative, i.e. to prove the legitimacy and objective validity of the categories.

§ 13 falls into three main parts. In part I (paragraphs 1–4) Kant explains the nature of a transcendental deduction by comparing it with an empirical deduction of concepts or with an empirical examination of the origin of concepts in the human mind. In part II (paragraph 5) Kant underlines the fact that a transcendental deduction is as necessary for the categories as it is for the concepts of space and time. In part III (paragraphs 6–8) Kant emphasises the difficulty of a transcendental deduction of the categories.

Résumé

If we wish to penetrate to the ultimate source of the concepts available to us, we must distinguish between an investigation which is to explain the origin of a concept (from experience) and an investigation which is to prove the legitimacy, i.e. the objective validity, of such a concept. The first kind of investigation may be called an empirical deduction, the second a transcendental deduction. An empirical deduction can be carried out in the case of empirical concepts; in the case of *a priori* concepts only a transcendental deduction is possible. *A priori* concepts form experience and cannot thus be deduced from it, though their accidentally arising in the mind of an individual person can be empirically, i.e. psychologically, explained.

A transcendental deduction of both the concepts of space and time and the categories is indispensable to proving their legitimacy within certain limits and their inadequacy outside those limits. For it is precisely this illegitimate use of the concepts which has so often led to empty and futile speculations.

Of course, a transcendental deduction of the categories is an extraordinarily difficult task. Although it is easy to see that formed reality can exist only in space and time, yet we still readily tend to assume that formed reality can exist independently of our own thought.

Explanation

FIRST FOUR PARAGRAPHS It is scarcely necessary to add anything to the résumé of these four paragraphs, except perhaps to say that Kant, although paying tribute to Locke's pioneer work, none the less disputes the applicability of Locke's method to *a priori* concepts.

FIFTH PARAGRAPH Kant here stresses the necessity of a transcendental deduction of the categories and of the concepts of space and time. He then goes on to discuss the misuse to which these two kinds of concept have been subjected. Newton and his successors were guilty of misusing the concepts of time and space (by making the concepts of space and time refer to things-in-themselves); the Leibnizians were guilty of misusing the categories (by making them apply to things-in-themselves; cf. commentary to §§ 7 and 8). In short: the transcendental deduction is necessary in the same way that the critical investigation itself is necessary.

SIXTH AND SEVENTH PARAGRAPHS In these two paragraphs Kant compares the transcendental deduction of space and time with the transcendental deduction of the categories. It is this seventh paragraph which has been the main occasion of the misunderstandings mentioned above. Kant has this to say: it is easy to understand that space and time are involved in all our representations and that there can be no object outside space and time. What is less easy to grasp is that the categories are also involved in all our representations and that there could be no object independently of the categories. In other words, Kant is posing his problem. It is conceivable that space and time should be determinate in themselves and that their determination should be neither logical nor conceptual. It is conceivable that phenomenal reality should be other than conceptually organised; it is, for example, conceivable that we could intuit bodies without at the same time conceiving them with their properties of extension, divisibility, etc.; it is conceivable that we could intuit changing nature without at the same time conceiving that it changes in accordance with necessary law (the law of causality). This account, in which Kant characterises his problem, has been misinterpreted: it has been construed as an account of a theory standing in direct contradiction to the critical theory which maintains that everything we represent (intuitively or conceptually) is formed through our understanding by means of the categories.

Grammatical. First sentence [first and second sentences] of the seventh paragraph (A 89/B 122): '*die Kategorien des Verstandes stellen uns gar nicht die Bedingungen vor*' ('the categories of the understanding, on the other hand, do not represent the conditions under which objects are given in intuition'), etc. The word *vorstellen* ('represent') does not here have its usual significance. The sentence means: the categories do not *adhere* to objects in the way that time and space almost visibly, as it were, adhere to them. The words *können* ('may') and *müssen* ('need') in the first (second) sentence and *können* ('can') in the second (third) sentence are *subjunctive*, as the subjunctive *enthielte* ('contain') shows. Kant is obviously following a well known rule of Latin grammar.[1]

'Intuition stands in no need whatsoever of the functions of thought' (A 91/B 123). Objects in space and time are what they are, namely, objects, through determinate space and time. That is to say: the objects of intuition can be completely described as such, namely, in terms of spatial relations and temporal context, e.g. as measurable, triangular; as enduring, changing, etc. We do not need a logical expression to describe an object of intuition as such,

[1] The verb 'posse' is used in the indicative even in conditional clauses.

i.e. we do not need to conceive a spatial object as a substance composed of inherences, or changing nature as changing according to causal laws, in order to intuit either as unitary entities.

Finally, in the eighth paragraph Kant argues against Hume that the concept of necessity cannot be separated from the concept of causality. He concludes that Hume should either have explained natural changes without recourse to the concept of causality or he should have realised that natural changes are necessary (and consequently that a transcendental deduction of the concept of causality is necessary).

SECTION 14

Introductory

In this section Kant is primarily concerned to explain (1) that there is only one satisfactory solution to the problem of cognition or knowledge—the solution based, namely, on the theory that phenomenal reality is formed by the human mind; and (2) that proof of this theory is to be found in the fact that any object of intuition, as an object of experience, can be described logically, i.e. conceptually (paragraphs 1 and 2).

The first two paragraphs of this section are already to be found in the first edition. In the second edition, however, the concluding sentences of the second paragraph have been omitted and three new paragraphs added. The last of these paragraphs is of especial importance for the transcendental deduction in its final version (see below).

Résumé

We describe the object of experience and thus of knowledge as matter formed by the human mind. The faculty of representation we describe as object-forming. However, it must be remembered that our faculty of representation is here understood in a comprehensive sense, namely, as containing the faculties of sensation, intuition and conceiving. Now, it has already been shown that, in a sense, our faculty of intuition (though not our faculty of sensation) possesses formative force. The question now arises: is it only our faculty of intuition which exercises a formative function, or does perhaps our faculty of conception also exercise a formative function in a still more basic sense? This question must be answered affirmatively: our faculty of conception does fulfil such a formative function, for any object of intuition, as an object of our experience and knowledge, may be described conceptually, i.e. categorically. But this simply means that the categories are universally applicable to the whole domain of possible experience, that no object of intuition (object of our experience) would be possible without the categories.

Explanation

FIRST PARAGRAPH The first two sentences (of the German text) ought to be read as one: the fullstop before *Entweder* ('Either') should be read as a comma.[2] Kant, totally rejecting the theory of pre-established harmony, seriously considers only two possible solutions to the fundamental problem of all Western philosophy: the relation of thought and reality. The two solutions which Kant seriously considers are: either thought imitates reality (Being), or thought forms—constructs—(phenomenal) reality.

The first solution is in Kant's opinion the solution of both the classical philosophers and the modern empiricists; the second is his own. Kant regards the first explanation of the possibility of knowledge as untenable, since, on its basis, reliable knowledge of nature (the certainty of mathematical and physical laws) and fruitful, i.e. non-tautological, logic would be impossible. The truth of the second explanation, i.e. the truth of the critical theory, will be proved in what immediately follows.

[2] The proposed alteration would scarcely affect the translation of the two sentences. [*Translator's note.*]

Fourth sentence. On 'sensations', cf. commentary to §§ 1 and 19.

Fifth sentence [*fifth and sixth sentences*]. This sentence contains the critical idea that our faculty of representation, while not creative in the full sense of the word, is creative in the sense that it forms matter.

Sixth [*seventh*] *sentence and the rest of the paragraph.* The object of intuition is, as we have already proved, formed through space and time—indeed, regarded in itself, it *is* determinate space and time. However, an object of intuition can become an object of experience; this simply means that every object of intuition can be described in logical terms. It follows that the reality we represent is not independent of thought, that without thought there could be no object of intuition (object of experience).

This is the transcendental deduction of the categories in a nutshell. Kant refers to this passage in the first edition of the Preface A XVII (cf. 'Introductory' to §§ 13 and 14). It is this passage which has so frequently been misunderstood. It is not Kant's intention here to 'prove' that concepts are the foundation of our conceiving; nor does he intend to say that concepts are given to us in and with objects; nor does he here maintain that the object of intuition is independently formed through space and time and is merely somehow co-ordinated with the category-based object of experience. What Kant in fact says is that the human mind, by means of the categories, formatively generates the object of intuition and thus the object of experience (knowable phenomenal reality).

The proof can, as Kant says, 'in any case [*allenfalls*] suffice by itself'; but the full deduction contains more than this. Here Kant proves only that unified representations and their object (the concept and the object of intuition) coincide and agree; but in the full deduction he will prove the perfect unity of conception and intuition; he will refer to a medium which, unlike space and time, does not stand between matter and conceptual form, but contains space and

KANT'S TRANSITION

time; mere matter; and also conceptual spontaneity. Consciousness is the medium in question.

Kant will then be in a position to show that the act by means of which we represent the object—intuitively or conceptually—is identical with the act by means of which we determine the consciousness, i.e. is the act by means of which we organise space and time, and through them the whole of nature in accordance with the category (cf. commentary to the 'Transcendental Deduction of the Categories', especially §§ 16–20).

SECOND PARAGRAPH In this paragraph Kant merely sums up the conclusions of §§ 13 and 14.

The phrase '*a priori* concepts' includes the elementary categories and the 'predicables'—logical, mathematical and physical.

THIRD AND FOURTH PARAGRAPHS In these two paragraphs Kant compares his philosophy with the theories of Locke and Hume. He explains that he wishes to attempt to steer a middle way between the theories of Locke and Hume in order to avoid their mistakes.

LAST PARAGRAPH OF § 14 (B 128 f.) The last paragraph of this section, which first appears in the second edition, prepares the ground for the argument of the 'Transcendental Deduction of the Categories' in its final form, and in particular for the argument of § 20, which contains a reference to this present paragraph (cf. commentary to § 20).

At the same time this paragraph in a way contains a summary of the metaphysical deduction, or, as one might also say, it adds the finishing touches to the metaphysical deduction. It does so by working out, with the greatest clarity, Kant's distinction between judgement and category, between mere logic and transcendental logic. The argument is terse and precise to a degree unusual even in Kant.

The crucial idea in this paragraph is that mere logic is incapable of constructing phenomenal reality; only logic combined with metaphysics is capable of this.

In other words, Kant maintains that the human mind, confronted with the indeterminate, although capable of generating conceptual unity and conceptual relation through its logical function, is incapable of achieving more than this. The relation S–P, as it occurs in a categorical judgement, may serve as an example. This relation is to be construed as a union of two concepts, of which each can be integrated into the other. The two judgements 'all bodies are divisible' and 'some divisible things are bodies' (others are triangles), regarded merely formally, illustrate such a relation. For if we assume that the two concepts partially or completely overlap in content—as they must in a true judgement—then the two concepts 'bodily' and 'divisible' can be integrated into each other (what is bodily includes, *inter alia*, what is divisible, and what is divisible includes, *inter alia*, what is bodily). That is to say: the two concepts of a judgement $S=P$ in so far as they overlap are—from a purely logical and formal point of view—the same as each other and can be substituted for each other.

Our merely logical function is incapable of producing any further determination; i.e. from a logical point of view the two concepts are indistinguishable. The purely logical act is, so to speak, a movement of thought, not bound to place; only formally determined as relation; it is, as it were, synthetic unity continually resolving itself anew into synthetic unity.

Thus it is only by means of the category that the human mind is capable of transforming mere relation or movement of thought into an object and thus fixing a starting point for future movements of thought. The category of substance is nothing other than the formal relation S–P realised in time; i.e. it is nothing other than an enduring whole consisting of co-existing parts; it is an intuitable representation, a synthetic unity established as object.

Hence it is only with the help of the category that it is possible to make a formal distinction between the two concepts of the bodily and the divisible (understood as one as far as content is concerned). We distinguish the two concepts by making the one refer to substance and the other to inherence, or—to put it grammatically—by expressing the one as noun and the other as adjective. In other words, in so far as we subsume one of the two concepts under substance we give it the meaning of body, which involves divisibility; we thus convert it into a concept applicable to certain objects of our experience or by means of which an object of intuition is established.

In short: coherent thought applied to the indeterminate does not generate an object; it generates only conceptual unity and conceptual relation. But coherent thought, manifested in a pure—i.e. logically determinable and universally applicable—element, is coherent thought understood as constructive. Or, looking at it from the opposite point of view, it is (unified) thought established as an object of intuition.

The crucial second sentence asserts: the categories are concepts of an object in general; they logically determine that object so that it can be intuited. That is to say, the categories transform the given manifold into an intuitable logical entity. This sentence contains the real essence of what Kant wishes to argue here: namely, that the categories, not mere judgement, construct the phenomenal world.

Last sentence. 'Similarly with all the other categories'.

Quantity. The judgement 'Caius is mortal', where 'mortal' refers to all the representations implicit in the representation 'Caius', admittedly indicates the conceptual form of totality; but it is the category which first makes it possible to intuit totality of representations, namely as a something enduring in time. That is to say: the category which transforms the multiplicity of representations, given as succession, into something unified establishes the (intuitable) representation of totality.

Quality. The judgement 'soul–immortal' affirms by its form the reality of the soul, i.e. indicates the logical concept of reality; but it is the category which first makes it possible to intuit something real, i.e. the phenomenally real is first established by the category, which transforms the given manifold—the materially filled forms of intuition—into an enduring object.

Relation. In this connection, cf. Kant's example and the commentary above.

Modality. The judgement 'since *ABC* is a triangle, the sum of its angles is necessarily 180°' indicates, it is true, the logical concept of necessity, for in this judgement one concept generates another; but it is the category which first makes it clear how one concept (or judgement) can generate another concept (or judgement): namely, as a concept realised in determinate space and time which necessarily imposes the norms contained within it on what is given.

TRANSCENDENTAL DEDUCTION OF THE CATEGORIES

INTRODUCTORY

The transcendental deduction of the categories—the very heart of the *Critique of Pure Reason*—contains the critical theory, almost in its entirety, in the form of a closely woven fabric. Indeed, the deduction of the second edition may be regarded as Kant's most mature account of his theoretical philosophy in all its essential parts. Everything which precedes the deduction—the doctrines of the 'Transcendental Aesthetic' and the first part of the 'Transcendental Logic'—is here once more treated at the highest critical level. The final relation of these two parts of the *Critique of Pure Reason* to each other is here defined and their ultimate significance revealed. On the other hand, what follows the deduction—the discussions of the second part of the 'Transcendental Analytic' and of the 'Transcendental Dialectic' may be regarded as merely applications and amplifications of the basic doctrines of the 'Transcendental Deduction'.

In short: in the 'Deduction' Kant works out the final conclusion of his critical thought: the new unity of logic and metaphysics. Within the human consciousness, Kant maintains in the 'Deduction', logical spontaneity is united with spatio–temporally bound sensuous receptivity; logical spontaneity is thus able to generate a picture of organised nature necessarily obeying its laws.

The 'Deduction' of the second edition falls into two parts: §§ 15–23 and §§ 24–27. In the first part (§§ 15–23) Kant shows that self-consciousness is the consciousness of synthetic unity and synthetic spontaneity, and that the fourfold form of synthetic unity, the categories, is the means (of unification) necessary to any understanding confronted with a manifold of impressions and capable of forming a unitary picture of the source of its impressions, i.e. of a given nature. In the second part of the 'Deduction' (§§ 24–27) Kant shows that the categories do in fact convert the manifold of impressions with which we are presented—i.e. nature given to us in space and time—into objects.

Outline of the 'Transcendental Deduction'

§ 15. Kant argues that organised nature is both unity and (knowable) complexity; he enquires into the ultimate source of this complex unity.

§ 16. Kant shows that self-consciousness is the representation of my own consciousness spontaneously organising itself into synthetic unity.

§ 17. What we call an objective representation is the representation of our own consciousness organised into synthetic unity.

§ 18. The representation of organised consciousness is objective only in so far as it is a representation of organised time.

§ 19. The representation of organised consciousness (i.e. of the objective representation) is representation of logical unity.

§ 20. The representation of logical unity depends on the categories, i.e. on the necessary norms regulating the unification of the manifold.

§§ 21–23. The categories are the means of knowledge indispensable to any created understanding, i.e. to any understanding dependent on a given manifold. The categories, however, do not apply to things-in-themselves and we must assume that the intuitive intellect of the Creator has no need of them.

§§ 24–25. Kant explains how the human mind can affect itself, i.e. how my productive organs operate on and determine space and time, and how they are able to generate determinate representations including the representation of my (phenomenal) Self.

§§ 26–27. Kant concludes that the categories determine the nature we perceive; they thus legislate for nature.

It is the second edition of the 'Deduction' which is explained in detail in this commentary.[1] The second edition contains no modification of Kant's theory as presented in the first edition. But in exposition it is clearer and its argument is not only unitary but also more cogent than the earlier version. In the first edition the whole 'Deduction' is divided into a subjective and an objective deduction; sometimes Kant argues from the empirical to the *a priori* and sometimes he argues in the opposite direction from the *a priori* to the empirical. By contrast, the second edition of the 'Deduction' is unitary: what is explained and proved from different viewpoints in the first edition is transformed, in the

---

[1] The first 'Deduction' has been assiduously studied and frequently explained and the second 'Deduction' largely neglected since Rosenkranz, under the influence of Schopenhauer, made the original 1781 text, rather than Kant's final 1787 version, the basis of his edition of the *Critique of Pure Reason*. Vaihinger's theory that Kant's thought went through various stages of development and contains many contradictions rests basically on an analysis of the first 'Deduction'. The existence of the second 'Deduction' was an uncomfortable fact for the proponents of this widely held theory. It was, after all, scarcely likely that Kant, in imitation of himself, as it were, should merely reproduce the various stages of his development along with all its contradictions. Still less was one willing to admit that in the second 'Deduction' Kant had arrived at a definitive and consistent view of his own philosophy. As a result, the second 'Deduction' was almost completely ignored. It was regarded as inferior to the 1781 version, which, it was emphasised, contained Kant's original inspiration. On the other hand, in a commentary like the present one, which is based on the assumption that it is possible to show the unity of a philosopher's thought, the second 'Deduction' must be made the basis of the interpretation. If Kant had a clear and coherent picture of his philosophy and if he tirelessly strove to improve its presentation we must conclude that the more mature version of the 'Deduction' is likely to be the superior version, i.e. the account which makes the unity of Kant's thought more clearly recognisable and more easily intelligible.

second edition, into a single line of argument proceeding from the *a priori* to the empirical.

It seems to me that the second edition contains everything to be found in the original version; indeed, the very expressions and turns of phrase to be found in the first edition reappear in the second.[2] I hope, therefore, that the reader will be able, with the help of the present interpretation of the second edition, to explain the text of the first edition for himself.

SECTION 15

Introductory

In § 15, which is really the beginning of the 'Transcendental Deduction', Kant shows (1) that all connectedness or combination in objects is based on acts of synthesis and (2) that the basis of all synthesis is the representation of synthetic unity (to be generated by the transcendental apperception). The basic problem of the 'Deduction' outlined in § 15, or rather the new and crucial standpoint from which Kant presents his philosophy in the 'Deduction', may be explained in the following terms. Kant looks at objective nature from two different points of view: (1) that of objectively, i.e. necessarily connected, nature; (2) that of nature spontaneously united by valid synthesis. The unity in this double conception rests on the doctrine that consciousness can be organised, i.e. that consciousness is a multiplicity of given representations which can be transformed into a unitary representation.

Résumé

In the present section, which serves as introduction to the 'Transcendental Deduction', we start, so to speak, from the beginning again.

We construe the human mind as creative, not in the full

[2] A notable exception is the term 'affinity', which is absent from the second version. Its function is taken over by the two terms *Objekt* ('object') and *Verbindung* ('connection').

sense, but in the sense that it is capable of forming the unformed; we describe the unformed as a manifold of representations given as succession and referring to three-dimensional form; we can also describe the unformed as spatio–temporally bound matter which elicits various sensations in us. Our spontaneous faculty of thought we characterise as formative.

We further construe the related (or unified) manifold as an (objectively) connected manifold; alternatively, we characterise any knowable connection of phenomena as an objective connection: hence we describe thought as connective, or more precisely as synthetic (for thought forms space and time, cf. § 10).

However, the concept of objective connection or synthesis must be thought of as depending on the possibility of synthetic unity, i.e. as depending on the possible occurrence, or 'producibility', of synthetic unity. Thus, we now investigate the possibility or original occurrence of (synthetic) unity. We shall find that (synthetic) unity is originally generated in consciousness, that it is originally realised as consciousness organised in accordance with the categories.

Explanation

FIRST PARAGRAPH *Introductory*. Kant is now in a position to explain the ultimate significance of his new and original philosophy. Here at last, therefore, appears the basic critical distinction (of form as opposed to matter) under its essential aspect, namely, of an original (necessary) act of determination. In other words: Kant now treats space and time as indeterminately given elements and represents *all* acts of determination—whether of space and time or of spatio-temporally bound matter—as acts performed by the understanding.

First sentence. Pure multiplicity of representations, which includes forms of intuition—i.e. sensations which (1) are either successive or in some other way multiple and distinguishable and (2) refer to something external, whether

KANT'S THEORETICAL PHILOSOPHY

spatial or not—belongs, as indeterminate intuition, exclusively to receptivity.

Second sentence [second, third, fourth and fifth sentences]. On the other hand, all connection of different representations—even the representation of pure spatio–temporal connection—is attributed to spontaneity of thought. Such spontaneity of thought can refer to a pure manifold of representations or to already formed concepts; it can refer to a multiplicity of pure spatio–temporal representations or to representations of spatio–temporally bound matter. For in each case the understanding generates determinate representation by transforming indeterminate representations or already formed concepts into conceptually graspable representations of determinate space and time. Such spontaneous activity of the understanding must always be construed as an act of synthesis.

Terminological. The expression 'not sensible intuition' means 'pure intuition'; it is not to be confused with the term 'non-sensible intuition', which means 'intellectual intuition' (cf. § 23, second paragraph).

Third sentence [sixth and seventh sentences]. The synthetic activity of the understanding is in essence and origin one: it is the action by means of which we transform many representations into a single representation. It is the only action of which the understanding is capable, and it includes its counterpart, analysis. In other words: the activity of the understanding can, in a way, be exhaustively described as synthetic activity (cf. 'Kant's reform of logic' II).

SECOND PARAGRAPH. *First sentence.* Connection involves (1) something to be connected: a given manifold of representations; (2) synthesis: the action of connecting; (3)—and this is a point which Kant emphasises—the concept of unity (cf. commentary to the third sentence).

Second sentence. What we call connection is in fact the representation of the united manifold, i.e. of synthetic unity.

TRANSCENDENTAL DEDUCTION

Third sentence [third and fourth sentences]. It is the representation of (synthetic) unity, therefore, which first makes possible the representation of connection; connection in itself is merely indeterminate, i.e. possesses neither form nor quality. That is to say: the traditional view maintained that unity could have infinitely many forms which depended on infinite (empirical) possibilities or forms of connection. But in the critical philosophy, connection has no form or quality of its own; its form has to be determined—indeed, connection first becomes possible through the form of unity.

Fourth and fifth sentences [fifth and sixth sentences]. The unity of which we are speaking is not, however, the category of unity; we are not talking about 'quantitative unity'. For the category of unity is itself already a united manifold, or a unity generated by synthesis. It thus depends on the possibility of valid connection (the ultimate source of which we have still to investigate).

'Qualitative unity' is defined in § 12 as 'unity of concept', etc. Qualitative unity is a whole which can be variously though uniformly described, i.e. it is the concept in general understood as synthetic unity. Quantitative unity is the concept of number in general understood as one of the forms of synthetic unity.

Sixth sentence [seventh sentence]. The unity of which we are talking is thus qualitative unity, i.e. the originally generated unity of which one can say that it is this unity which first makes possible any connection produced by judgement (and hence by the conceiving understanding). Our concern now is to discover this highest unity. We shall find its origin in the human consciousness, where it is spontaneously generated.

KANT'S FOOTNOTE TO § 15 Kant adds: as long as we are concerned with the indeterminate, synthesis is all-embracing, and the question of analysis cannot arise at all. For, looked at from this point of view, we are not concerned with representations as already formed concepts (implying other concepts) but with consciousness as a manifold, i.e. as consciousness capable of being variously organised; we are thus concerned with various still-to-be-formed concepts.

'(potential) consciousness' is organisable consciousness, for consciousness first becomes consciousness by being organised (cf. § 16).

It is possible that the note is also intended to dispose of a potential objection, namely that even obvious tautologies are described by Kant as syntheses. (In connection with this objection, cf. commentary to § 19.)

SECTION 16

Introductory

This section contains the crucial doctrine of the 'Deduction' —indeed, of the *Critique of Pure Reason* itself. In order to prove that the human understanding legislates for nature, Kant here maintains that phenomenal reality is nothing other than the content of human consciousness; that, as a result, self-consciousness or the spontaneous representation of one's own Self may be construed as the action by means of which we 'create' both ourselves and the whole of nature; we do so, namely, by forming what is unformed.

This act, Kant maintains, is produced by the apperception. Apperception, as a human 'prime mover', organises nature by organising our own consciousness; it 'creates' both phenomenal nature and our phenomenal Self by determining what, for our receptivity, is a mere manifold of spatio–temporally bound sensations. In short: Kant maintains that self-consciousness is a faculty through which we represent not only *one* consciousness but universal unity; and that, since such unity is generated by synthesis, phenomenal reality is nothing other than my own consciousness spontaneously organised according to the logical principle of synthetic unity.

The Cartesian basis of Kant's philosophy is here quite unmistakable. Descartes was the first to make 'truth' depend on man, the first to derive the certainty of reality from consciousness or thought. However, Descartes based only the existence of the thinking subject on the thinking consciousness. The existence of nature, and ultimately of the Self too, still depended on the existence of God. Kant, however, strictly differentiates between knowledge of reality on the one hand, and absolute truth on the other. He maintains that knowledge is based exclusively on man and his cognitive organs, while absolute truth is totally inaccessible to us. Kant shows (1) that the certainty arising from thought (or self-consciousness) refers as much to nature as to my Self, i.e. refers as much to the object as to the subject; (2) that such certainty pertains only to phenomenal reality, never to absolute truth.

Kant therefore wishes to show that the Self, understood as the content of thought, is synonymous with the phenomenal nature constructed by thought; and that the Self, understood as the thinking subject, is the spontaneity which constructs both nature and the Self through logical synthesis.

In order to prove his theory that thought 'creates' both nature and the Self, Kant starts from what is given, i.e. intuition; he describes it as a manifold of representations synonymous with a unitary representation. In order to show that the uniform representation (intuition) is ultimately the representation of the synthetic unity realised in consciousness, Kant analyses consciousness and finds in § 16 that (1) the unitary representation which coincides with a manifold of representations is representation of *one* consciousness; (2) the principle of the unitary consciousness is a principle imposed by the mind on itself; (3) the imposition of this principle must be understood as an act of spontaneous synthesis.

The argument of the first part of the 'Deduction' (§§ 16–20) may also be summed up as follows. Even if nature is described as mere intuition—i.e. as a manifold of representations coinciding with a *single* consciousness—we can still show (1) that our representation of nature and the Self is spontaneously formed; (2) that the form is synthetic unity (§ 16); (3) that synthetic unity is objective, logical and categorical in character (§§ 17, 19 and 20).

The present section § 16, which proves the spontaneity of the human mind, is perhaps the most profound and most influential piece of writing in the whole of German literature —indeed, in the whole history of philosophy. This passage shows that the organisation of nature is in truth the genesis of nature carried out in our own consciousness. The static concept is here transformed into a dynamic function; and it clearly emerges that the act of thinking is truly a creative act. The simplicity of Kant's proof is admirable. From the single fact of man's self-consciousness he derives the doctrine that man possesses a faculty which is legislative for nature, i.e. from the single fact of man's self-consciousness, Kant infers the whole critical philosophy with all its ramifications.

Résumé

FIRST PARAGRAPH From self-consciousness follows the creative faculty of the human mind: this creative faculty is the means by which the whole of nature and the phenomenal Self is formed.

Each one of our representations can be construed in two ways: (1) as representation of an object; (2) as part of the Self. Representation, understood as intuition, may be described as any given manifold capable of being transformed into unified consciousness, i.e. can be construed as the pure and original matter of apperception which is transformed into the pure and original form of apperception. Thus if we are able to represent the Self, it is because each of our representations is both consciousness of an object and consciousness of unity *vis-à-vis* the manifold.

SECOND PARAGRAPH Such consciousness of unity *vis-à-vis* the manifold must be consciousness of unity *arising* from the manifold, i.e. self-consciousness ultimately turns out to be consciousness of the synthetic genesis of nature. For were it not the case that all our representations were both represen-

TRANSCENDENTAL DEDUCTION

tations of an object and consciousness of the object coming into being, we should be unable to distinguish between the Self and the non-Self; i.e. it would be impossible for us to be conscious both of the identical subject and of objective nature. But since it is obvious that given nature cannot itself possess the property of synthetic and formative spontaneity, it follows (from the fact that we are self-conscious) that the human mind, by generating its own conscious Self, is alone responsible for generating the phenomenon of organised nature.

THIRD PARAGRAPH It must, however, be emphasised that nature, known or capable of being known by us, can be regarded only as a phenomenon and not as a thing-in-itself.

If we construe every representation of synthetic unity as coinciding with human consciousness organised by synthesis, we may also speak of a non-human mind or consciousness which does not organise itself by synthetic acts but which creates itself and the universe by merely becoming conscious of itself. That is to say: whereas the Self of which we are conscious as a spontaneous force is only form for which nature supplies the content, we can also speak of a Self which is completely raised above form and content; the self-consciousness of such a Self involves the creation both of itself and of the universe.

Explanation

FIRST PARAGRAPH *First sentence.* For a representation to be possible I must be capable of being conscious of my Self as its subject. If this were not the case the representation would not be a (potential) part of my consciousness, and only that of which I can be conscious exists for me.[3] That is

---

[3] The first sentence of § 16, or rather a misinterpretation of it, would appear to have been the starting point from which certain of Kant's successors set out. Kant was interpreted as follows. Everything which exists must exist for my consciousness. What exists for my consciousness

to say, any representation can be described (1) as its content or object and (2) as my own representation or as part of my consciousness. In other words: I am able to distinguish between my Self-as-subject and nature-as-object, in spite of the fact that the representations of which my Self is composed have exactly the same content as the representations of which nature is composed.

Second and third sentences. Even intuition, which is the representation of an object still to be determined and which can thus be construed as a manifold of representations—even intuition, then, can as such become part of my own consciousness. The critical philosophy views intuition as a manifold which is unity. It is the task of the 'Deduction' to explain how the manifold and the unity can be the same. It explains this fact by means of the doctrine of the unitary consciousness.

Fourth sentence. None the less, the representation of my own consciousness ('this representation') is neither given nor sensible; it must therefore be spontaneous. That is to say: whereas the representation, objectively understood, is given and sensible, subjectively understood, it is necessarily spontaneous. In other words: the distinction which can be made

---

must be thinkable, must be conceivable. It would then follow that the thing-in-itself, which cannot be conceived, cannot exist (Maimon) or that thought and the Being realised in history and nature are the same (Hegel). But what Kant is really maintaining is this: whenever I am conscious of an object I am also potentially conscious of myself as thinking subject; i.e. (formative) thought is contained in each of my representations referring to phenomenal reality. Human consciousness, according to Kant, is spatio-temporally bound: it is a manifold of representations given as succession and referring to three-dimensional form. The thing-in-itself may exist for a different kind of intellect—say, the divine intellect—thought of as independent of space, time and any given manifold and as self-creating in creating objects. For our consciousness, however, the thing-in-itself is merely something negative. That is to say: categorical thought attaches to the phenomenal reality it generates; but categorical thought is not connected in any determinable way with Being, which it is incapable of grasping (cf. commentary to 'Phenomena and Noumena').

between the subjective and objective sides of the representation is also necessarily the distinction between sensibility and spontaneity. Differently expressed: this distinction which embraces even intuition makes it possible for us to construe any representation as spontaneous.

Fifth sentence. This representation of my own consciousness ('it' refers to 'this representation') is to be called pure apperception. That is to say: if representation in general is construed as subjective, i.e. as self-consciousness, it is construed as spontaneity operating on some given manifold. It is thus understood as an intellectual medium, i.e. as a given manifold which is transformed into intellectual form; it is thus also understood as unity in general—and this is always to be construed as coinciding with my own consciousness.

It may also be called 'original apperception', since the unity contained in or generated by it is the ultimate unity, the representation, namely, of universal unity containing all other representations within itself. (On empirical apperception or apprehension, cf. commentary to § 26.)

'Apperception' is a Leibnizian term signifying conscious perception, i.e. a process uniting in itself both perception and logical activity or, more precisely, clarification. It is therefore both receptive and spontaneous. Similarly, the critical term 'apperception' signifies a consciousness embracing receptivity and spontaneity. However, in the critical philosophy, receptivity relates only to what is indeterminate; and spontaneity is not clarificatory but synthetic and formative. Thus the term 'transcendental apperception' contains Kant's novel doctrine that a spontaneous and logical transformation of the manifold into synthetic unity precedes all empirical perception ('apprehension'). This process is independent of all empirical matter. By its means are generated the forms or archetypes in accordance with which all empirical perception takes place. (Cf. also Kant's discussion of 'apperception' in the first edition of the 'Transcendental Deduction', A 123 f.)

I now add the following explanation of pure or original

apperception: it is the mind, understood as a validly constructive faculty, i.e. as the faculty which creates phenomenal reality by organising a consciousness (viz. any manifold of representations) in accordance with the categories.

Sixth sentence. The unitary representation spontaneously generated in this way shall be called the 'transcendental unity of self-consciousness'. It is the unitary representation of consciousness in general; this unitary representation coincides with the determinate representation in general, the archetype or the pattern of all empirical representations.

Seventh sentence [*seventh and eighth sentences*]. That the unity of consciousness is both fundamental and formative emerges from the following consideration: it is only because a manifold of representations occurs within the medium of consciousness that it is possible for these representations to constitute a unitary whole for me (i.e. can exist for me); or: for representations to exist for me, i.e. for representations to be determinate they must fulfil a certain universal condition: namely, conversion into synthetic unity. Were this condition not fulfilled, they could not be part of my consciousness.

In other words: the representation of my own consciousness is nothing other than the representation of a unitary intellectual medium, i.e. the distinction which can be made between the objective and subjective sides of any representation is in fact the distinction between the object, on the one hand, and unity *vis-à-vis* the manifold, on the other.

Eighth sentence [*ninth sentence*]. We can draw an important conclusion from this combination of unity and multiplicity in consciousness (cf. commentary to the next sentence).

SECOND PARAGRAPH *Introductory*. Kant has reached the ultimate goal of his investigation. He is now in a position to present his final conclusion: the doctrine of the 'necessary (synthetic) unity of apperception', which he describes as 'the highest principle in the whole sphere of human know-

TRANSCENDENTAL DEDUCTION

ledge'. In other words: Kant offers, as the final result of his critical investigation, the doctrine that all human knowledge is knowledge of phenomenal reality validly constructed in accordance with the necessary principle of synthetic unity.

Kant's doctrine or ultimate principle may also be explained as follows: the very essence of all that we know is logical relatedness or logical unification spontaneously generated by the human mind through the media of space and time.

First sentence. The distinction between nature and the Self, which relates to all our representations, and which, as has been shown, involves consciousness of unity *vis-à-vis* the manifold, is ultimately the distinction between the object and its synthetic genesis. Self-consciousness, on the other hand, is nothing other than consciousness of organised nature coming into being.

Second sentence. Representations of (empirical) unity, which coincide with consciousness of determinate unity, do not enable us to make that distinction. That is: self-consciousness cannot be originated empirically; the identity of the Self cannot be experienced *a posteriori*. Just as it is impossible to experience the principle of causality by means of which natural phenomena are connected, so is it impossible to derive from experience the principle or form by means of which many representations are united: the principle or form of the *single* consciousness. The principle or form of the single consciousness is rather imposed on representations (spatio–temporally bound sensations), and that by the mind understood as apperception.

Third sentence. It is not consciousness of determinate or constructed unity, but consciousness of unity being determined or constructed within my Self, which enables me to distinguish between the Self and nature; i.e. self-consciousness can only be generated transcendentally.

Fourth sentence [*fourth and fifth sentences*]. Self-consciousness is thus consciousness of the many representations which are transformed into a unitary representation. Hence the representation (the concept) of the identical Self ('the analytic unity of apperception') depends on an antecedent synthesis, namely, the transformation of many representations into the unitary representation of organised nature ('the synthetic unity of apperception'). That is: self-consciousness turns out to be the faculty by means of which we, in determining our Selves, create organised nature.

This fourth sentence contains the very heart and core of the 'Deduction'—indeed, of Kant's philosophy in general. Kant is here saying that self-consciousness involves not only the reality of the thinking spontaneous subject (which is what Descartes teaches, according to Kant) but also the reality of objective and phenomenal nature (including the phenomenal Self). For the act of self-representation involves (1) a given manifold, and (2) a universal principle of spontaneous thought, namely, synthetic unity. In other words, Kant is maintaining that what for us is the original representation of unity is at the same time the representation of knowable nature with all its basic laws; that our mere faculty of representing determinate unity is actually our faculty of knowing the whole of nature through its fundamental laws.

Fifth sentence [*third paragraph, first, second and third sentences*]. Kant first of all sums up by saying that consciousness of an intuition, construed as consciousness of part of my Self, can only mean that I am conscious of the emergence of unity from the manifold. He then adds the following negative proof: if it were impossible to distinguish between the representation of the object and consciousness of its synthetic genesis, self-consciousness would also be impossible, i.e. the representation of the object and the Self, which are identical in content, would be exactly the same.[4] For I represent my Self by becoming conscious of the outer and inner intuitions

[4] It is conceivable that this sentence constituted the starting point of Fichte's philosophy. The distinction between the Self and the non-Self, understood as the ultimate form of all distinction whatever, is for Fichte the metaphysical foundation of all knowledge and all reality.

which are or have been given to me—intuitio..
in which I live, of the jouneys I have made, o.
of pleasure or pain which I am experiencin̹
experienced. These intuitions, and the concepts ᵢ
them, are the exclusive content of my consciousness.
in addition to such representations, I can be conscious ᴄ
(thinking) Self only if I become conscious of the poᵥ
manifested in these intuitions. But this power—which ᵢ
constant, while the intuitions are variable—can only be my
spontaneity operating on what is given by forming it (for
it is incapable of creating it).

Sixth sentence [*third paragraph, fourth sentence*]. The unity
arising from the manifold can thus be construed as the
foundation of self-consciousness and hence of all my
objective representations too, since, as far as content is
concerned, the latter are identical with my representations
of my Self. The identity of the Self thus depends on the
synthetic genesis of my objective representations.

Kant is not saying here that the representations of the
Self and those of organised nature mutually condition each
other. What he is maintaining is that we can distinguish
nature from the Self only because we are able to impose the
principle of synthetic unity on any given manifold and thus
'create' reality, albeit only phenomenal reality.

Seventh sentence [*third paragraph, fifth, sixth and seventh
sentences*]. Kant now calls the synthetic unity of representations realised in nature, i.e. objective representations,
'connection' (or, to use the terminology of the first edition,
'affinity'). He goes on to draw the conclusion that such
connection, i.e. knowable connectedness (cf. commentary
to § 15) can be construed only as a product of the human
understanding. This latter must therefore be regarded as a
faculty of original or productive connection, i.e. as the
faculty of spontaneously transforming a given manifold of
representations into a *single* consciousness (unified representation). Finally, Kant characterises the doctrine of
objective connection, i.e. the doctrine of the organisation

of nature by means of synthetic spontaneity operating on a given manifold, as 'the highest principle in the whole sphere of human knowledge'.

KANT'S FOOTNOTE TO § 16 In this note Kant definitively proves that analytic unity is always merely secondary and dependent on synthetic unity. He does so by showing that the representation of the Self is as little something absolute as the analytic unity of the concept; the representation of the Self rather belongs to appearance and is no more 'real' than the synthetic nature upon which it depends. The representations of a property, understood as a unifying characteristic, i.e. a general concept like 'red', depends on the synthetically unified consciousness. In other words: the representation of a property depends on determinate representations of objects (e.g. roses) which are represented as having, among other things, the property 'red'—i.e. these objects are logically unified by means of the concept 'red'. If such a representation is to be a general concept it must be applicable to yet-to-be-determined representations, i.e. applicable to a manifold capable of being transformed into a unity. Thus the representation of a unifying property depends on the fact that it is possible to organise consciousness synthetically.

It follows that the representation of my *merely thinking Self* is not ultimate but derivative. The representation of a property applicable to a manifold depends on the possibility of organising nature synthetically. (The representation of such a property may, incidentally, be understood in two ways: (1) objectively: as general concept; (2) subjectively: as consciousness of my conceptual faculty or as the representation of my thinking Self.)

In this way Kant proves that all logical or analytic unity, at which one arrives by abstraction and which was regarded by the Leibnizians as ultimate and original, is only secondary, since it depends on the realisation of (categorical) synthesis. It thus follows, to use Kant's own words, that 'the synthetic unity of apperception is therefore the highest point', i.e. the faculty of organising consciousness synthetically 'to which we must ascribe all employment of the understanding, even the whole of logic', i.e. all analytic thought, and 'conformably therewith, transcendental philosophy. Indeed, this faculty of apperception is the understanding itself'.

THIRD PARAGRAPH [*fourth paragraph*] *Introductory.* Kant here shows that the unity of form and matter underlying what we call organised nature is merely phenomenal in character. It is therefore possible for us to conceive an intellect transcending form and matter; the creative act of such an intellect does not unite form and matter but creates them simultaneously.

First sentence. 'This principle of the necessary unity of apperception is itself, indeed, an identical, and therefore analytic proposition' (cf. § 17, paragraph 4, where this remark is repeated).

This principle is analytic in the Kantian sense of the word because the concept of reality or existence (which are both categories) involves the concept of the condition of possibility. This latter concept can be construed in Kantian terminology as one of the pure derived concepts of the understanding, one of the so-called 'predicables' (cf. § 10).

I trust it will be permitted me to add the critical remark that here, more clearly than anywhere else, Kant reveals the limits of his logic. It is precisely because he does not recognise synthesis as the form of speculative thought that his synthetic logic, although applicable to the natural sciences, is not applicable to the historical or moral sciences (cf. also p. 28).

Second sentence. Although self-consciousness is possible for us, it is possible only as consciousness of spontaneity in action. The content of our representations of the Self refer, however, to external nature, which is transformed by synthesis into unified consciousness.

Third sentence. For a (divine) intellect, intuition and conception are the same; in contemplating itself it would create both itself and the universe. But our intellect can only conceive, i.e. can only connect what receptivity makes available to us; in the full sense of the word it creates neither itself nor the universe.

This is the first of Kant's many allusions to the divine intellect and the positive noumenon, allusions which are to be found scattered throughout the 'Transcendental Deduction' (cf. especially the commentary to §§ 21–23 and also to the chapter 'Phenomena and Noumena'). It may be mentioned here that Kant's concept of the divine intellect shows the unmistakable influence of Aristotle's *deus contemplivus*. But whereas Aristotle's God contemplates forms, Kant's God transcends both form and matter. Kant's God neither contemplates (i.e. does not intuit) nor thinks, but acts in a way which for us is quite incomprehensible. It is, of course, true that we can paradoxically characterise the divine activity as intuitive thought or conceptual intuition, but these notions are meaningless for us. And if we say that God, in creating the universe, creates himself by a single and for us unintelligible act, this only serves to show that all differentiations and conceptual distinctions are merely human in character, and that we can have no concept or knowledge of identity and difference in those spheres which are for ever inaccessible to our powers of comprehension.

On Kant's doctrine of the Self as mere form, cf. commentary to § 25.

Fourth sentence. Self-consciousness, in the human sense, is thus consciousness of unity arising from a given manifold.

Fifth sentence. The conclusion which Kant draws amounts to a summary of § 16: self-consciousness is ultimately consciousness of original synthesis. The principle of the single (synthetic) consciousness is thus a necessary and all-embracing principle. An act of synthesis is always necessary if a given manifold is to become part of my consciousness, i.e. is to exist for me.

TRANSCENDENTAL DEDUCTION

SECTION 17

Résumé

FIRST PARAGRAPH We have already said that all our unitary representations (intuitions) are representations of spatio-temporal unity. We now say: all our representations, both intuitional and conceptual, are representations of synthetic unity.

Our consciousness is organized by synthesis and each of our intuitions and conceptions can be construed as coinciding with organised consciousness, i.e. with synthetic unity.

SECOND PARAGRAPH We now turn to the explanation of the concepts 'knowledge' and 'object'. What we call an object is nothing other than the representation of one's own unified consciousness. The object is the representation of something determinate; ultimately nothing is given except a mere manifold of representations; all determination is based on synthetic acts; these acts of synthesis unite consciousness and generate determinate representations. We can thus assert that the representation of the single consciousness is the representation of the object, i.e. the objective representation which is the basis of knowledge.

We thus describe the object and consequently all our knowledge as *valid construction*. All our knowledge is based on representations of determinate unities. But there can be nothing determinate for us except what we synthetically construct in space and time, i.e. what we validly construct. It is in this sense, then, that we characterise knowledge, which always refers to objects, as synonymous with valid construction.

For the remaining paragraphs see 'Explanation'.

Explanation

FIRST PARAGRAPH Kant begins by summing up his position: he refers to the limiting conditions which are imposed on us (1) by the given media or intuitional forms of space and time, (2) by the necessary form of all constructive thought, namely, synthetic unity. The first kind of condition concerns the manifold given in intuition; the second concerns all determinate representations, since they refer to the organisation of the consciousness in general.

KANT'S FOOTNOTE TO § 17 Kant argues that space and time themselves as pure unities are subordinate to the principle of the single consciousness. He says: space and time are pure intuitions, i.e. unitary representations, coinciding with the manifold in general. As a result, they are not merely concepts, i.e. special representations implying other representations; they are rather any given manifold which is transformed into unitary consciousness; they are thus synthetic and yet ultimate.

In harmony with his position throughout the 'Deduction' (cf. commentary to § 15, paragraph 1), Kant (1) describes the indeterminate consciousness in terms of a consciousness involving the indeterminate forms of intuition; (2) the determinate consciousness he describes in terms of a consciousness coinciding with the unitary representations of space and time. That is to say, in the 'Deduction' space and time are described as given not *to* but *with* consciousness. It follows that the unitary representations of space and time are spontaneously and synthetically generated; on the other hand, originally organised consciousness, as synthetic unity, must be understood as coinciding with the unitary representations of space and time. Kant adds that 'The *singularity* of such intuitions is found to have important consequences'.

Textual. I regard the reference to § 25 at the end of the footnote as mistaken. It seems to me that Kant is referring to § 24 (paragraphs 4–6) rather than to § 25. In § 25 the Self is treated largely as pure spontaneity, while in § 24 it is treated exclusively as an appearance. The combination of the present footnote and § 24 constitutes a continuous argument: since the unified representations of space and time are products of synthetic spontaneity it follows that

TRANSCENDENTAL DEDUCTION

the Self, which we are capable of knowing, can only be phenomenal. Kant's first footnote to § 26, which, like this present footnote, discusses the relative share of receptivity and spontaneity in generating the unified representations of space and time contains a reference to § 24. One final remark: it is quite conceivable that in the course of preparing the second edition of the 'Deduction' Kant hesitated some while before eventually deciding on the point at which to divide §§ 24 and 25.

SECOND PARAGRAPH *First sentence.* In order to prove that knowledge is valid construction, Kant explains: (1) that the understanding can be generally characterised as the faculty of knowing;

Second sentence. (2) that knowledge consists in making representations refer in a definite way to objects;

Third sentence [*second sentence*]. (3) that the object is a manifold of representations conceived as synthetic unity.

Fourth sentence [*third sentence*]. Kant repeats that the transformation of a manifold of representations into unity is actually the organisation of consciousness.

Fifth sentence [*fourth sentence*]. Kant concludes: the act by means of which consciousness is organised, i.e. the act by means of which various representations are transformed into one *single* representation, generates the representation of the object, i.e. the representation of something which can be both conceived and intuited. This act thus converts representations into objective representations and therefore makes them the foundation of all knowledge; it is this act which first makes possible the use of the understanding.

Kant is here offering the solution to the problem posed in the introductory section of the 'Transcendental Analytic': how is agreement between representations and their objects —how is knowledge—possible? It is possible, he maintains, because objective nature is the product of the human mind, which by its logical function transforms the matter given to

153

the senses into (spatio–temporal) entities, i.e. into objects which can be both intuited and conceived.

THIRD PARAGRAPH Kant here repeats his final conclusion that everything we represent is necessarily 'created' as synthetic unity by ourselves. Thus, for example, space as something given to us is indeterminate—it is merely an infinity of possible relations within three-dimensional form. Knowledge of space is thus always 'creation' or valid construction. It always consists in the realisation of synthetic unity. Any such act of realisation is determination of the consciousness. The synthesis of representations is hence the 'creation' of an object. Such creation is determination of what is indeterminate. It follows that nothing determinate exists apart from what is created by my own act—the act by means of which I organise my own consciousness.

FOURTH PARAGRAPH The highest principle—the principle of the objective validity of the synthetic unity of apperception—is analytic. It makes the organisation of consciousness a condition of the possibility of all determinate representations; hence it amounts simply to the fact that the consciousness of my thinking Self is possible only as consciousness of the object which is thought, i.e. of the synthetic unity arising in thought (cf. also § 16, paragraph 3, sentence 1).

FIFTH PARAGRAPH This paragraph represents a detailed repetition of § 16, paragraph 3, sentence 3. The only new point here is the concept of sensible intuition unlike our own spatio–temporal intuition. This problem, one of the most subtle of the transcendental philosophy, is discussed in detail by Kant at the end of the first part of the 'Deduction', particularly in § 23 (cf. commentary).

I need only add here that in §§ 15–23[5] Kant wishes to prove that the category, i.e. logic, is valid for any intellect—not merely the human intellect—whose representations

---

[5] In §§ 24–27 Kant proves that the categories do actually determine given nature, i.e. materially filled space and time.

TRANSCENDENTAL DEDUCTION

depend on a given manifold. Only an intellect not dependent on a given manifold, the divine intellect, is free from the principle of synthetic unity, i.e. categorical logic.

SECTION 18

Introductory

In order to understand the purpose and meaning of § 18 we must remember that Kant's philosophy, understood as the union of logic and metaphysics, is so constructed that it must lead to a single master-concept and harmonise with a single representation, namely that of scientifically known nature. Since Kant builds his philosophy on a representation which is both necessarily as it is and yet also constructed by the human mind, he is obliged to work out a theory of error which explains the (empirical) possibility of non-valid construction. This would make possible the distinction between non-valid construction—the merely accidental association of representations—and valid construction, i.e. original synthesis. If Kant were unable, within the framework of the critical philosophy, to explain the occurrence of error, reality would appear, not as necessarily constructed, but as freely constructible. That is to say: known or knowable nature would not necessarily be as it is; it would be conceivable in various ways, depending on the subjective point of view.

The critical theory of erroneous judgement is given in the 'Transcendental Aesthetic', § 8 III, footnote. The critical theory of error, understood as non-valid or subjective construction, is contained in the present section.

In traditional logic, erroneous judgement is construed as the erroneous application of a concept to reality. A spurious or empty concept is understood as a concept neither derived from nor applicable to reality. In the transcendental logic, a valid judgement is understood as the integration of a representation into a yet-to-be-formed concept, or as the application of a conceptual relation to yet-to-be-formed nature, i.e. it is understood as the union of an empirical representation with a concept realised in space and time. Consequently, erroneous judgement is not construed as integration or union but as the mere combination of representations with already constructed objects; accordingly, an empty or non-valid concept is construed as the mere association of empirical representations—representations referring to already constructed objects—and thus as a representation which is not synthetic determination of time (cf. §§ 9–10).

According to the critical philosophy, unformed consciousness is originally nothing other than indeterminate time, while originally formed consciousness is synonymous with determinate time. The content of § 18 can thus be summed up as follows: the union of consciousness, as an act of determining time, is objectively valid, whereas the mere association of determinate representations, which cannot be an act of determining time, is accidental and merely subjective in character.

Résumé

We have said earlier that the object is nothing other than the representation of a determinate consciousness. We now add: whereas consciousness admittedly includes merely associative representations without objective validity, these subjective representations are merely derivative, i.e. are dependent on original objective representations.

Unformed consciousness is originally a pure manifold of (successive) representations; originally organised consciousness (the representation of an object) is such a manifold transformed into synthetic unity, i.e. organised time. On the other hand (empirical) consciousness refers to already constructed objects and is thus not consciousness of (necessarily) simultaneous or (necessarily) successive representations, that is to say, empirical consciousness does not coincide with organised time. It only reflects associated representations and thus has only subjective significance; as a result, its spontaneity is only secondary and not object-forming.

Explanation

First sentence. Kant is preparing the ground for his new distinction between the objective and the subjective unity of consciousness, i.e. between consciousness corresponding to validly constructed reality and consciousness which does not so correspond. This he does by describing the transcendental, i.e. objective, unity of spontaneous consciousness as the faculty or means through which a manifold of representations, given as succession and referring to three-dimensional externality, is converted into a unified representation (phenomenon as object). (Cf. § 17, paragraph 2.)

Second sentence. Subjective unity of consciousness, by contrast, is represented as the determinate inner sense, i.e. as my inner states in so far as no objective reality corresponds to them. Accordingly, the inner sense (as subjectively, i.e. secondarily, determinable) coincides with a manifold of representations referring to empirical, i.e. already formed, objects.

The inner sense is here described implicitly in empirical terms. The inner sense, understood transcendentally—i.e. in its ultimate critical significance—is discussed at length by Kant in § 24 (see commentary).

We must not forget the elementary foundation of Kant's theory: the appearances which we represent, the nature which we know, is nature reflected in our own consciousness. Accordingly, Kant maintains that everything we represent—whether it be a representation of a validly constructed object or a picture of things which do not even exist as we represent them—is always synonymous with the *unified* consciousness. In this way, Kant is able to distinguish two kinds of consciousness: that which corresponds to objective nature and is the same as an originally and categorically united manifold, and that which corresponds merely to a subjective representation of nature and is nothing other than variously associated representations.

Third sentence. A successive manifold of representations

referring to already formed nature may be represented by the mind either as simultaneous or as successive.

Underlying this sentence is the important critical idea that the principle of the (necessary) simultaneity or the (necessary) order of representations is not derived from experience but springs from the spontaneous mind.

Fourth sentence. Hence empirical consciousness, unified with reference to already formed objects, is not a synthetic unity but only an association of representations; it signifies the 'construction' of appearances on the basis of already constructed appearances and is thus merely accidental.

Fifth sentence. Now follows the crucial observation: objectively determinable nature is nature as time. Fully paraphrased, this runs: on the other hand, the pure manifold represented as unity is identical with the originally organised consciousness, since I cannot represent any unity except by representing the manifold as a *single* consciousness. Such representation is based on spontaneous synthesis, which generates a single consciousness (the original representation of synthetic unity) and, by this means, makes possible all representations of empirical synthetic unity, i.e. objective nature. In other words: the unformed (human) consciousness is ultimately only a succession of representations. As a result, all formed (determinate) representations are originally representations of determinate time, i.e. of an enduring element consisting of co-existent parts whose states necessarily succeed each other.

The words 'merely as intuition in general' contain an allusion to Kant's concept of a sensible intuition differing from our own (cf. § 23). 'Succession' is obviously the characteristic of our human kind of inner intuition, i.e. the way in which multiplicity is given *to us*. Whether there are other ways in which multiplicity may be given, i.e. may be intuited, and what these other ways may be, is something we can never know.

Sixth sentence. Only primary spontaneity, which organises time and thus consciousness, 'creates' objects (in general).

Empirical spontaneity is secondary; it depends on determinate representations of natural appearances (objects) and also on psychological factors.

Seventh sentence. Empirical spontaneity is subjective in the sense that different persons can connect 'ostensible' concepts, i.e. already formed concepts, with different 'things', i.e. already constructed appearances. Empirical spontaneity is unity of consciousness referring to already constructed objects and not determining time; it is thus not synonymous with nature, universally and necessarily organised. That is to say: empirical spontaneity is merely synthetic unity, not established as object; it is an effect of the reproductive imagination unifying representations in various ways on the basis of already formed objects.

I conceive only what I validly construct. Although I can represent something which I do not validly construct, I do not conceive it. I can have a word for my representation, but this word, since it is only applied subjectively to an already formed object, is not a validly formed concept, but a representation connected merely accidentally with an appearance; the appearance, on the other hand, is only subjectively characterised; it is not grasped conceptually. Thus, for example, I can have a word 'rose' for my representation of a certain flower; but unless I construct the object 'rose' as bloom, thorns and perfume, etc., necessarily co-existing together, I merely represent bloom and thorns in varying succession. I can thus connect the word 'rose' sometimes with this object and sometimes with that; no objective concept can ever arise from such association. Only by validly constructing the appearance of a rose as a substance composed of its inherences can I lay the foundation for the concept 'rose'. This conception, combined with other similarly formed conceptions, can become part of a system of scientific botany.

SECTION 19

Introductory

In § 18 Kant treated objective consciousness as the *a priori* foundation of all our representations, both objective and subjective. He described objective consciousness as a representation which is necessarily and universally valid for phenomenal reality, viz. as synthetic unity (or determinate time). In § 19 Kant treats objective consciousness not only as the *a priori* foundation of our representations but also comprehensively as the representation of organised nature itself (containing within itself the principles of its own organisation). At the same time, he shows that the act through which consciousness is organised and phenomenal reality validly constructed is an act of judgement, i.e. a logical act. This act may be described as (1) an act of unifying empirical concepts (§ 19) and (2) an act unifying the manifold by means of the categories (§ 20).

The importance of the present section is this: having shown that the human mind imposes certain necessary and universally valid laws on given nature (§§ 16 and 17) and, further, that the spontaneous act of unifying consciousness leads, under certain circumstances, to merely accidental and subjective results (§ 18), Kant succeeds in explaining in the present section (§ 19) to what extent the human mind gives nature its fundamental law without however predetermining nature in every particular and detail. In other words, he explains how the theory that nature is to be necessarily constructed may be harmonised with the principle of research based on observation; i.e. with the theory that nature is to be known objectively through experience. Kant takes the two empirical concepts 'body' and 'heavy' as examples and explains, within the framework of his logic of valid construction, how these two concepts may be objectively united without at the same time being necessarily united.

Kant's explanation is basically this: starting from the

accepted principle that mere induction cannot produce universally valid, necessary knowledge, Kant wishes to show that empirical knowledge is objective knowledge. He maintains that the unity of 'body' and 'heavy' is logical in character. This unity is based on our capacity to subsume a single phenomenon under different concepts: that is, this unity is based on our faculty of construing the indeterminate conceptually—more precisely, of construing the indeterminate by means of a higher order concept implying lower order concepts. Our empirical knowledge is thus knowledge in the strict sense of the word, i.e. it is objective knowledge, in so far as it is experience logically expressed or conceptually constructed. For experience becomes knowledge only by means of conceptual construction, i.e. it is only by means of conceptual construction that experience becomes a body of concepts or theorems systematically built up and capable of systematic development. On the other hand, knowledge of this kind is neither necessary nor universal, since it depends, *inter alia*, on sensations, i.e. factors which, for all we know, may be variable. (Both the matter within us and the matter outside us may, for all we know, change; gravitation, for example, might cease to operate.)

The present section is well suited for drawing a comparison between the philosophies of Hume and Kant.[6] What the sceptic can see only as a subjective connection of ideas or as an association of different observations, Kant is able to interpret as objective—though not necessary—unity and thus as a valid foundation for knowledge. We can also see in this section, however, the great importance of Hume for Kant with respect to his theory of substance. What Kant says about substance is, namely, the exact reverse of what Hume says.

According to Hume, substance is nothing other than the habitual and repeated association of certain ideas. Kant, while accepting the basis of this position—that substance is

[6] On the relation between Hume and Kant, see the commentary to § 26.

identical with representations and is thus contained in experience—maintains that the connection of such representations is by no means based merely on habitual association but rather contains the logical union of such representations, and thus, as an *a priori* representation, underlies experience. It then follows—in partial opposition to Hume—(1) that the representation of substance, since it is based on a principle arising from the understanding, is necessary and independent both of psychological accidents and experience; (2) that, although the representation or category of substance composed of its inherences is universally valid for experience, its empirical application in particular cases, where sensations are involved, leads only to non-necessary knowledge.

Résumé

The representation of the single determinate consciousness, explained above as the representation of the object and determinate time, in the end turns out to be the representation of logical unity. For consciousness referring to given nature coincides not only with many but with different representations. Hence the representation of a *single* consciousness, i.e. self-consciousness, is the representation of a unity which is also diversity.

Such unity is logical in character and is based on the functions of judgement or on acts which organise indeterminate consciousness by means of a conceptual relation, namely, that of the higher order representation implying lower order representations. Hence, although any particular act of unifying representations need not be necessary, none the less the act, which objectively (as representation of time) unifies the consciousness, also organises the indeterminate through a conceptual relation; it is thus a logical act.

Explanation

THE TITLE The logical form inherent in all judgements (acts of unification through synthesis) is the same as the objective unity of consciousness; this latter is understood as various concepts unified or as one concept involving others. That is, the objective unity of consciousness is logical—conceptual—unity.

FIRST PARAGRAPH The objections raised by Kant against the usual definition of judgement as 'representation of a relation between two concepts', are based, of course, on the opposition of his own logic to traditional logic.

Kant has two reasons for rejecting the traditional definition of judgement as 'representation of a relation between two concepts'. First: judgements are, as Kant says, in certain cases relations not between concepts but between judgements. This observation must have appeared important to Kant, since he derived the dynamic categories from those judgements (hypothetical and disjunctive) by means of which judgements, not concepts, are related to each other (cf. §§ 9 and 10).

Second: although the definition of a judgement as a relation may be adequate in traditional logic, transcendental logic requires that this relation should be determined, and determined as the relation of the higher order concept to the lower order concept which it implies (cf. 'Kant's reform of logic' II), and thus as objective unity of consciousness.

KANT'S FOOTNOTE TO § 19 Kant emphasises his objection to the logicians of the old school who reduce hypothetical and disjunctive judgements—so important for the critical philosophy—to categorical judgements.

SECOND PARAGRAPH *First sentence.* The critical definition of judgement is that it is the objective organisation of consciousness, the formation of a valid concept implying other concepts. Judgement is thus described as the act by means of which known phenomenal reality is validly constructed. That is to say: knowledge is here regarded from two points of view: (1) as known (conceptually unified) nature; (2) as unifying principle (judgement). Having strictly distinguished unification by judgement from merely subjective association, Kant finally interprets the objective organisation of consciousness as the (logical) unification of diverse representations.

Second sentence [*second and third sentences*]. Kant characterises the word 'is' as the linguistic symbol of objective unification, in contrast to merely subjective association (cf. sentence 6).

Third sentence [*fourth and fifth sentences*]. In this and the following sentence Kant explains the critical concept of objective knowledge based on necessity but not itself necessary. Knowledge based on or coinciding with conceptual unification is objective in character because (1) it is produced by an original act of organising consciousness and (2) such organisation of consciousness, namely, as determinate time (substance consisting of inherences), is based on necessity. That is to say: we originally, and thus validly, form the concept of the 'heavy body', for example, by constructing the concept out of our actual sensations, and that in the form of a substance consisting of inherences.

Fourth sentence [*sixth sentence*]. Although the representations of 'body' and 'heavy' are not necessarily united, although we can form the concept 'body' without thinking of it as being combined with the concept 'heavy', none the less, without some antecedent logical unification no knowable object would be represented. Therefore, the representation of any knowable object depends on the principles of (categorical) logic applied to time. For if experience is to become knowledge, it must be logically constructed; in other words, it must be one and the same with logically organised nature.

Kant thus maintains that we acquire objective empirical knowledge by unifying our sensations, that our sensations can be transformed into objective knowledge because they are given to us as a succession of representations capable of being converted into the representation of something simultaneous and enduring and thus into a concept. On the other hand, however, Kant also shows that empirical objective knowledge is by no means necessary or strictly universal. The reason is that what is here transformed into a unified representation (our sensations—the content of our successive representations) may, for all we know, be variable.

Fifth sentence [*seventh sentence*]. Judgements represent the logical organisation of consciousness by means of the unification of diverse representations, in direct contrast to mere association of representations.

Sixth sentence [*eighth and ninth sentences*]. For example, I can associate the two representations 'body' and 'heavy' without unifying them. For mere connection in perception does not produce unity. As long as I merely say, 'If I support a body, I feel an impression of weight', I am not objectively connecting the two representations 'body' and 'heavy'. They remain distinct. Only by forming the concept 'body' into a concept containing the representation 'heavy' do I generate a unified representation. The body is heavy—heaviness belongs to bodies—being bodily is being heavy; this logical mode of relating or unifying two—or more—representations by means of judgement generates a kind of representational unity which can be called objective.

It might be here objected—perhaps the objection has already been made—that Kant is artificially, even paradoxically, representing a tautology as a synthesis. The 'unity' of 'bodily' and 'heavy' is a matter of definition; unity is identity. 'Bodily' and 'heavy' are interdefinable. If I should ever come across a non-heavy body I should simply invent a new word for it, and the unity of 'bodily' and 'heavy' would remain a definitional unity fixed for all time.

It is, of course, true that the unity of two connected representations can be regarded as a matter of definition. Kant's trichotomy, analysis–synthesis–association can easily be reduced to the dichotomy definition–association. And yet, by introducing the principle of synthesis into logic, Kant effected the reform of logic which has often been regarded as his greatest achievement.

If one regards 'bodily' and 'heavy' merely as two words

applied to the object of a *single* observation, body, and equated with each other by definition, one overlooks or disregards the possibility that each of the two words may both refer to the whole of the observation, body, and yet signify different things. It was the significance of this possibility which Kant grasped and made the foundation of his new logic.

For 'bodily' and 'heavy' may be regarded not only as identical by definition, but also as mutually determining each other, i.e. as representations, each of which objectively adds something to the other; hence their (valid) connection can be interpreted as knowledge, viz. as a theorem, generally applicable and thus capable of being part of an existing and developing system of knowledge.

SECTION 20

Introductory

This section concludes the first part of the 'Transcendental Deduction' proper. Kant proves that the categories are necessarily valid for any intellect which finds itself confronted with a given manifold, i.e. for any intellect for which intuition and concept are *not* identical—irrespective of whether the media of intuition are space and time or some other media unknown to us.[7] Kant shows that a given manifold can be converted into a determinate representation only if the given manifold, unified in accordance with the *categories*, is converted into unified consciousness. It follows that the category is the foundation of all logic, and logic the foundation not only of conception but also of intuition.

In the second part of the 'Deduction', particularly §§ 24–27, Kant is at last in a position to show that the categories are actually valid for given nature, i.e. that the categories determine the appearance we call nature and therewith legislate for nature.

[7] The latter idea is discussed in §§ 21–23. This group of sections constitutes, to to speak, an appendix to the first part of the 'Deduction'.

Résumé

It has been shown above that the representation of a single consciousness is the representation of logical unity. It will now be shown that the determinate representation, whether concept or intuition, is always the representation of categorical unity.

Different representations referring to given nature are transformed into a *single* consciousness through the function of judgement, i.e. the unification of such representations is effected under the principle of the higher order concept implying lower order concepts. But such unification occurs according to certain necessary rules which can be universally described as the rules of determining time. Hence, if a given manifold is to be converted into a single consciousness (i.e. into a unitary representation), this must be effected in accordance with those universal rules, the categories.

Explanation

First sentence. Referring to § 17, Kant explains that the manifold represented as unity is nothing other than a single consciousness organised as synthetic unity.

Second sentence. Referring to § 19 (where the organisation of consciousness is described as logical union), Kant continues: whether such a manifold referring to given nature is understood as unitary representation (intuition) or as connected representation (concept based on *a priori* or *a posteriori* antecedent judgements), we can always describe the act by means of which consciousness is organised as a logical act and this, in its turn, as an effect of the function of judgement.

Third sentence. It follows: if a manifold of representations referring to given nature is to become a unified representation, the transformation must occur in accordance with the forms of thought inherent in judgement.

Fourth and fifth sentences. Since these forms of thought are nothing other than the categories, and since the understanding originally generates the unitary representations by applying the categories to a given manifold, e.g. time, it finally follows that the transformation of a given manifold into unity must always occur in accordance with the categories.

At the end of the fourth sentence Kant refers to B 128 f. § 14 and not, as Vaihinger thought, to § 10. Although it is true that the argument of § 10 is necessary to an understanding of the present section, Kant none the less emphasises here, in particular, that judgement, as a merely logical function, does not 'create' reality. It is rather the category which first makes possible the unitary representation of given nature; it does so by originally realising logical form in a medium, e.g. time (cf. commentary to § 14). Kant there shows that what creates reality is not logic by itself but logic applied to a given medium, i.e. transcendental logic (or logic united with metaphysics).

At this crucial point a new attempt at explaining Kant's theory of the valid construction of phenomenal reality through logical spontaneity may be welcome.

Consciousness is a manifold of representations. For the human mind this is successiveness; *in abstracto* it is mere multiplicity.

Consciousness is a manifold of representations referring to an intuitable externality. For the human mind, this externality is space; *in abstracto* it is merely intuitable externality. Externality in and for itself is indeterminate and unformed; no lines are drawn in it, no limits are marked. But all that this means is that the many representations which constitute our (possible) consciousness are representations of an indeterminate externality, not intuition of objects. It is thus the spontaneous organ inherent in our consciousness which 'creates' something unified and intuitable. For in spontaneously converting the given manifold of representations into a unified representation (implying an infinite number of determinable representations), it transforms the indeterminate unlimited entity into something formed. This something formed is, so to speak, constructed within or hewn out of the unlimited. Things formed in this way confront us in intuition as unities. These, then, are products of our ordering synthetic faculty of representation.

Kant has been frequently misinterpreted as maintaining that there would be no reality if there were no people to have representations of it, or as maintaining that reality is as it is because the human mind represents it in this way. A rose, for example, would not be what it is—or would not exist at all—if the human mind did not exist. But what Kant really says is different. It is true that Kant starts from the idea—which incidentally is of pre-critical origin—that the reality we talk about is the reality reflected in our own consciousness. But this idea is only the foundation upon which Kant builds his system. What he is really saying is this: if the rose were not an appearance validly constructed by ourselves but rather a (divinely) given thing-in-itself, it would necessarily be a different thing for each individual, and each individual would form his own 'knowledge' of roses according to his own (sensible) experience—an uncertain 'knowledge' based on an insecure foundation. Therefore we can only describe the rose as phenomenally real. Only in this way is it possible to understand how I can have an objective representation of a rose. Only on the assumption that I logically, i.e. necessarily, construct within the given media of space and time the indeterminate (material) source of my sensations of light, shade, colour, etc., as 'rose' is it possible to understand how I can objectively intuit a rose and acquire knowledge on the basis of my various representations referring to given nature (cf. also commentary to § 26).

SECTIONS 21–27

Introductory

In the first part of the 'Transcendental Deduction' (§§ 15–20) Kant proves that the categories are subjectively real and objectively valid. He shows that what we call self-consciousness is, in the last analysis, our conceptual faculty, i.e. our (logical) faculty of unifying a given manifold in harmony with the twelve rules or forms, the categories. In the second part Kant proves that the application of the categories is necessary. That is, he shows that the categories necessarily refer to the appearances which together we call nature.

SECTION 21

Résumé

FIRST PARAGRAPH The categories, as explained, are rules regulating the unification of the manifold. A unified manifold is logical unity realised in human consciousness. But what has so far been disregarded is the fact that the manifold is given to us as a succession of representations referring to three-dimensional space. It will be shown in what follows (particularly in § 26) that the unity before us in experience is in fact the category manifested in the materially filled forms of intuition, i.e. is logical unity.

SECOND PARAGRAPH None the less, it has already been clearly shown that for any intellect, apart from God's, nature must be construed as something indeterminately given, for it is only as such that it can be determined by logic. The divine intellect, on the other hand, gives itself the determinate and does not need logic to unify the manifold or to determine what is given.

Explanation

FIRST PARAGRAPH *First sentence.* Kant summarises the content of §§ 15–20: consciousness of the unity of my Self is consciousness of the unified manifold. I realise the categories by means of the act which unifies the manifold (§ 20).

Second sentence. Just as the empirical unity of intuition is dependent on the pure unity of intuition, so is empirical consciousness based on pure consciousness, i.e. on the categorical unity of the original representation.

KANT'S FOOTNOTE TO § 21 In the text Kant merely asserts that self-consciousness is identical with consciousness of categorical synthesis. In the footnote he offers the following proof of this. Synthesis is representation of unity; but unity is the representation of the unified manifold. The faculty by means of which we unify the manifold is called apperception. Any unity represented by us is thus a unified manifold; it is therefore logical unity or unity of apperception.

SECOND PARAGRAPH *Last sentence.* Kant here draws the limit which the critical investigation may not hope to cross. Admittedly it is possible to prove (1) that we determine by logical action, (2) that the indeterminate is given to us not only as matter or sensations, but also as mediating representations, i.e. as forms of intuition inherent in human nature. But it is impossible to explain why all thought is limited to the traditional forms of judgement and consequently to the twelve categories, nor why space and time are the only mediating representations possible for us.

Kant, in full awareness of the whole compass of his thought, indicates the point at which his rational considerations stop and his metaphysical assumptions begin.

We may here add that Kant's philosophy—the philosophy of phenomenal reality formed by the human understanding in accordance with necessary laws—contains at least three implicit assumptions which are now regarded as either outdated or doubtful:

1. Kant's description of organised space assumes that Euclidean geometry is the only possible geometry.
2. Kant's conception of knowledge or science as applied logic presupposes that a certain traditional system of twelve judgements is the only possible logical system, and, as a consequence, that all thought is necessarily bound to the twelve categories he describes.

3. Kant's conviction that all natural change is law-governed assumes that the concept of causality is the only concept by means of which natural change can be described as law-governed (cf. also p. 171).

SECTIONS 22 AND 23

Introductory

The two §§ 22 and 23 are closely connected. They are intended to prove that the categories, either by themselves or in combination with any intuition other than our own, do not yield knowledge, and that, *vis-à-vis* noumena, they are utterly meaningless. In § 22 Kant shows (1) that the categories, as a means of unification, require a given manifold, and (2) that the unifying categories, when merely applied to pure intuition, produce no knowledge of any kind. In § 23 Kant shows (1) that although the categories are applicable to any kind of intuition, i.e. to any manifold intuitable in any medium, this extended application of the categories still cannot lead to any new knowledge, and (2) that the noumenon has no relation of any kind to the category. It follows that only in combination with the empirical intuition given to us in space and time do the categories lead us to knowledge.

SECTION 22

Résumé

Although the categories determine pure intuition, this can lead only to formal 'knowledge', i.e. to empty concepts. For pure intuition is merely something imaginary. Intuition is given to us as filled intuition. Space and time do not in themselves exist; they exist only as nature. As a result, even if the categories can be applied to pure space and time, we are still unable to acquire transcendent knowledge; on the contrary, our knowledge is limited to nature understood as space and time, i.e. to appearances.

TRANSCENDENTAL DEDUCTION

Explanation

The divine intellect thinks (creates) unity; the human intellect unifies by thought. For the divine intellect, thought *is* knowledge; for the human intellect thought is only one of the two conditions of knowledge: the other condition is the given manifold capable of being transformed into unity. Such a manifold as pure multiplicity is admittedly given in space and time. But thought which refers merely to this pure manifold—as is, for example, the case in mathematics—cannot lead to 'knowledge'. Such thought is rather merely a construction of unity out of multiplicity in accordance with the rules of logic.

Kant here wishes to emphasise that mathematical knowledge cannot be regarded as transcendent knowledge, and indeed that mathematical knowledge which does not refer to three-dimensional nature would be empty and fruitless —not knowledge at all.

According to Kant, all knowledge is applied logic. Mere logic is empty and fruitless. Mathematical knowledge is logic applied to space. But if mathematics referred only to mere space it would be as empty as mere logic. Space as such, namely, does not exist; it exists only as materially filled space, i.e. as three-dimensional nature. Kant is thus here maintaining that pure mathematical construction, if it were inapplicable to three-dimensional nature, would be empty and fruitless. In maintaining this position, he shows how dependent he was on the mathematical and scientific knowledge of his time.

SECTION 23

Introductory

The importance of this section consists in Kant's observation that logic is valid not only for our phenomenal nature but for any nature whatever in so far as it is given to the senses only as a manifold. That is, the critical conception of logic is that it is quite independent of both the factors of human psychology and all material conditions whatever. It is valid for any created intellect, i.e. for any intellect which does not create by knowing.

For any non-divine intellect, whether human or otherwise, the only means of acquiring (objective) knowledge is synthetic categorical logic. For it is only by means of logic that the manifold can be unified, and for a created intellect only the manifold is given, and it remains unknown until it is transformed into unity.

Résumé

FIRST PARAGRAPH The category must be applicable to any sensible intuition, not merely a spatio–temporal intuition. For us, however, the manifold and hence the object can only be spatio–temporally represented. It follows that no knowledge can arise from the applicability of the category to non-spatio–temporal intuition.

SECOND PARAGRAPH The concepts 'category' and 'object' become completely meaningless *vis-à-vis* non-sensible intuition. These concepts are significant only with respect to an already formed or still-to-be-formed manifold. But for the intuitive understanding there is no difference between the manifold and unity, and it therefore has no need of the categories. Again, everything which the intuitive understanding intuits is objective, and thus the distinction between the objective and the subjective also disappears. A category which is applicable to any sensible intuition is therefore totally meaningless with respect to intellectual intuition. But knowledge arises only from the application of the category to what is given to us in our sensuous intuition, i.e. in space and time.

Explanation

FIRST PARAGRAPH The categories are valid beyond the limits of our own spatio–temporal intuition; they are valid for anything given sensibly. That is to say: everything given sensibly must first be categorically unified before it can enter a single consciousness.

However, the categories detached from our media of intuition are for us merely empty forms; we can say nothing either about the possible occurrence of other media or about the occurrence of objects in media unknown to us. For, in any other medium, the categories would not appear as something enduring and three-dimensionally formed; but how they would appear we cannot say. It follows that the categories, although ideally applicable beyond our intuition, are not actually so.

Penultimate sentence [sixth and seventh sentences]. '*die jene allein enthalten*': the word *die* is accusative and refers to the synthetic unity of apperception; the word *jene* is nominative and refers to the categories. [Kemp Smith's translation reads: 'which constitutes the whole content of these forms'. It should read: 'they (the categories) constitute the whole content of it (the synthetic unity of apperception)'.— *Translator's note.*] The categories, and they alone, represent the synthetic unity of apperception. If the categories are not realised there is no synthetic unity of apperception, i.e. we represent nothing.

SECOND PARAGRAPH Even if we assume the existence of things-in-themselves, we still have no faculty which enables us to know them. Our inferential intellect can, it is true, tell us what properties of appearances cannot possibly attach to things-in-themselves; but it is not in a position to determine the thing-in-itself positively. Negatively, however, the following radical and exclusive determination, so to speak, may be given: not even the categories can be applied to the thing-in-itself. Thus for example: our concept of substance is absolutely dependent on a given manifold; it signifies the unity generated out of the manifold. It is thus a representation into which other representations are thought of as inserted, but which for its part cannot be thought of as insertable into a representation since it is a totality. As a result, it can only be the subject, never the predicate, of a sentence.

Leibniz had made knowledge of substance an attribute of God. Kant, however, shows not only that substance lies within the human faculty of knowledge (and in this he follows Hume) but also that it is precisely the divine intellect which does not need to know anything about substance.

'But of this more hereafter': this is doubtless a reference to the chapter 'Phenomena and Noumena' and particularly to the passage A 241 ff./B 300 ff.

SECTION 24 I

Introductory

The section consisting of §§ 21–23 is something of a digression. Kant there proves that the logic of the categories is valid not only for the objects of human experience but also for the objects of any experience whatever. Only those objects which the divine creator simultaneously thinks and creates lie outside its scope. In §§ 24–26 Kant returns to his main theme and proves in this concluding part of the 'Deduction' that our highest faculty, apperception, does really determine all the objects which appear to *us*. Kant first shows—in § 24—that our spontaneous logical faculty, valid for any given manifold, i.e. for original matter, does really order and determine the original matter given to *us*, namely, time— and therefore also space. In § 26 (after another digression composed of § 24 II and § 25) Kant finally proves that the objects actually confronting us in our varied experience are 'created' by our spontaneous faculty operating through the categories; he proves, in other words, that such objects are simply the intuitional forms of space and time materially filled and determined in accordance with the categories.

Résumé

FIRST PARAGRAPH As explained above, the categories applied

to the manifold in general do not result in knowledge. The concept of the unified manifold in general—which is also the concept of the object in general—does not enable us to represent determinate objects. Only because we can become conscious of the manifold as a succession, only because our many different representations are given to us as successive representations, is it possible for our spontaneous faculty to generate something determinate, i.e. objects. The object arises because we transform representations given to us in an indeterminate order into the representation of something enduring which consists of co-existent parts and whose states succeed each other in a determinate order.

SECOND AND THIRD PARAGRAPHS The unification of a manifold in general is called 'intellectual synthesis'. The transformation of an indeterminate succession into duration, simultaneity and determinate succession is called 'figurative synthesis'. The mind, understood as the faculty of figurative synthesis, is called 'productive imagination'. As such it mediates between sensibility and the intellect and, though wedded to sensibility, is to be regarded as a transcendental organ.

FOURTH, FIFTH AND SIXTH PARAGRAPHS The spontaneous organs inherent in the human mind (understanding and productive imagination, both of which are subsumed under apperception) must be strictly distinguished from the inner sense, which is not a spontaneous organ. The inner sense is rather determined by apperception; by itself the inner sense is merely a manifold of (possible) representations, and even the successive character of this manifold can only be seen and conceived by us through a synthetic act of the understanding.

As a result, the representation of my Self, which is nothing other than the total content of my inner sense, is based both on my spontaneity and on time as the form of my inner sense.

KANT'S THEORETICAL PHILOSOPHY

Explanation

FIRST PARAGRAPH *Introductory*. The first two sentences sum up §§ 21–23. The third sentence contains the central idea of § 24, which is also one of the crucial ideas of the critical philosophy as a whole. The idea in question is this: our spontaneous organ generates formed, thinkable and representable objects—i.e. substances with their inherences which are also perceivable—by operating on an indeterminate succession of representations (indeterminately given time).

First sentence [*first and second sentences*]. Although it is true that the categories are applicable to any sensible intuition (our own as well as any other), i.e. are applicable to any given manifold, none the less, regarded in the abstract, i.e. regarded as referring to a medium other than our own, they establish no object but are merely forms of thought.

Second sentence [*third and fourth sentences*]. Looked at in this way, the categories are merely the characteristics of the act of thought or the properties of the synthetic process; that is to say, they are purely intellectual and are incapable of becoming (describable) objects.

Third sentence [*fifth, sixth and seventh sentences*]. But for us space and time are given as the forms of our intuition. (As has been explained, intuition can be construed as merely received, and space and time as 'primary matter'; cf. commentary to the 'Transcendental Aesthetic' and to § 15.) Hence *our* inner sense is consciousness as a succession (manifold) of representations; the inner sense in general, however, is consciousness as a multiplicity (manifold) of representations. As a result, by transforming a given succession into duration and simultaneity, the understanding is capable of determining our inner sense in accordance with the synthetic unity of apperception, not only *in abstracto* as a unified manifold, but also *in concreto*. Thus our understanding constructs enduring substance, which consists of co-existent inherences, as the necessary archetype of anything perceptible. Thus, through the operation of the understanding on time, categorical unity (the manifold unified in accordance with the categories) becomes objectively, i.e. phenomenally, real.

SECOND AND THIRD PARAGRAPHS Having expounded his doctrine that the logical categories are ideally valid beyond the sphere of human experience (§ 21–23), Kant now goes on to describe the human mind, or the actions of the human mind. He does so from two different points of view, describing the mind by two different names. The mind, understood as a conceptual faculty ideally valid outside human experience, is called understanding; the action of the mind in this sense is called intellectual synthesis. The mind, understood as a faculty which is valid only for and yet also creatively determinative of human experience, is called productive imagination; the action of the mind in this sense is called figurative synthesis.

That is to say: if the concept of the understanding is to be limited so that it signifies only the logical faculty, it will be necessary to regard the mind from a different point of view, viz. as productive imagination. Looked at in this way, the mind is not merely the faculty of abstract logic; it is an organ which realises logic in appearance and which originally generates phenomenal unity. Hence productive imagination, although indissolubly connected with sensibility, is nevertheless one of the transcendental organs.

In a sense, productive imagination is the most characteristically Kantian of the organs. For it is by its means that the peculiarly critical combination of logic and metaphysics is brought about. It converts the logical act, which unifies the manifold, into a metaphysical act which establishes phenomenal reality.

Kant scholars have maintained that the concept of the productive imagination was formed by Kant only at a late stage of his philosophical development. Indeed, Kant has even been accused of not having understood the deep significance of his own doctrine and of having carelessly abandoned it soon after he had conceived it.

The concept of productive imagination, whether the mind is described by this name or not, is one of the crucial concepts of the critical philosophy. Even if it were granted that Kant developed the term relatively late, and even if it were true that the subtle discussion of the capacity of the intellect respecting a sensible but non-spatio–temporal intuition is a late addition, all that we could infer from this would be that Kant had found at this late stage a new way of presenting his thought, not that he had evolved a new philosophy. On the contrary, his philosophy remained unchanged from the moment it was conceived, i.e. from the moment he was able to see it as a unified, all-embracing system.

SECTION 24 II

FOURTH PARAGRAPH Kant has now completed his discussion of the different spontaneous faculties inherent in the human mind, and is at last in a position to offer a definitive account of the two closely connected doctrines of the inner sense and the Self as appearance. The problems associated with these two doctrines have already been touched on several times before, particularly in the 'Transcendental Aesthetic', §§ 6, 7, 8 II.

As is known, the concept 'inner sense' originally comes from Locke. Kant redefines the term and introduces it with a new meaning into his system. Admittedly, for both Locke and Kant inner sense is a receptive organ. But whereas for Locke a receptive organ is capable of receiving determinate impressions, in the critical philosophy impressions which are *merely* received (by the human mind) are always indeterminate. For this reason Kant carefully distinguishes inner sense as a receptive—or mediating[8]—organ from the spontaneous organs inherent in the mind: apperception, the

[8] Cf. Kant's doctrine of the inner sense and the Self as phenomenon. See p. 184.

understanding and productive imagination. The term inner sense, in its most subtle Kantian significance, is nothing other than an indeterminate manifold of representations. Even the awareness of the successive arrangement of these representations presupposes a spontaneous act of synthesis (cf. Kant's first footnote to § 26).

Just as we can become aware of the three-dimensionality of space only by drawing three lines at right angles to each other from a given point, so also we can become aware of the successive nature of time only by moving through the successive points of a line.

Successiveness, understood as the unity of a line, i.e. as a series or a number, is a determinate representation based on the category of quantity (cf. 'Schematism', A 145/B 184). But in the last analysis the only thing given to inner sense is a manifold of possible representations—a multiplicity—capable of being grasped as successiveness.

Kant's definitive account of the Self as phenomenon is also contained in the second part of §§ 24 and 25. In the light of the discussions in §§ 21–23 Kant investigates possible knowledge of the Self from three points of view. In §§ 21–23 he distinguished three kinds of thinkable object: (1) pure form manifested in pure intuition (in space and time); (2) pure form manifested in a non-spatio–temporal medium; (3) pure form manifested in empirical intuition, i.e. in spatio-temporal nature. Accordingly, Kant now investigates our possible knowledge of the Self (1) as pure spontaneity, (2) as something manifested in a non-temporal medium; (3) as temporal appearance. He finds that we can know the Self only as a temporal appearance.

The two sections §§ 24 and 25 must be understood as Kant's definitive refutation of the Cartesian philosophy of Being. It is here that he finally refutes Descartes' basic doctrine that self-consciousness involves the absolute reality of the Self. As far as a divine or self-creative intellect is concerned, it is admittedly conceivable that, by mere thought, it should know (and create) its own Self and the whole of nature. The human, i.e. created, intellect, however, requires something more than spontaneous thought to know either its Self or an object; it needs matter given to the senses.

The basic Cartesian doctrine thus involves an illusory metaphysics. The fact that I am conscious of my Self is by no means a proof of the absolute reality of the Self. On the contrary: self-consciousness is consciousness of my spontaneous faculty, and hence of my capacity to represent both my Self and nature as appearances.

FIFTH PARAGRAPH *First sentence*. The spontaneous faculty of unifying the manifold determines the inner sense.

Second sentence [*second, third and fourth sentences*]. The understanding, as a purely logical organ, is incapable of intuition and is dependent on sensibility and hence on time as the form of sensibility. It is just because the understanding depends on time as the form of sensibility and possesses no form of its own that the pure acts of the understanding are empty. None the less, it is possible for the understanding to affect time. For the inner sense, understood as some kind of manifold, e.g. as succession, is ordered by the understanding; that is to say, the manifold inherent in the inner sense is transformed into determinate unity.

Third sentence [*fifth sentence*]. Thus the understanding—which can now be called productive imagination—operates on the mind (of which it is the organ) by affecting (determining or ordering) inner sense.

Fourth sentence [*sixth and seventh sentences*]. Apperception is construed as an organ which (ideally) unifies any given manifold, and not merely the spatio-temporally given manifold. But inner sense is nothing more than a manifold of representations (given as succession), i.e. inner sense is time as indeterminate intuition. It is only because the mind consciously performs an act of synthesis that determinate intuition as self-consciousness is possible.

SIXTH PARAGRAPH *First and second sentences* [*first, second, third and fourth sentences*]. The synthetic character of all our spatial representations, even the simplest and most elementary, is most clearly apparent from the fact that we cannot represent anything determinate in space without constructing it. Nor should the synthetic character of our representations of time (as ordered succession) be doubted, for we can represent ordered succession only by means of a spatially constructed figure, namely, that of a drawn line (cf. § 6, paragraph 2; also the explanation to § 24—the present section—paragraph 4).

Third sentence [*fifth sentence*] *and the first footnote*. Ordered succession may be described as movement, and movement as the synthetic determination of space, and hence time.

Kant here introduces the term 'movement', not in the sense of movement of thought in general, but in the sense of an action of the productive imagination. Such an action, says Kant, orders time by determining external nature. That is to say: productive imagination generates ordered time by realising time in space; it transforms indeterminate succession into ordered succession by converting space into the spatial unity of a line.

Movement, as an action of the productive imagination, thus mediates between space and time. Movement is transcendental in character, for, ultimately, it is the pure logical forms, not ordered time, which productive imagination, by its movement, makes manifest in space.

Fourth sentence [*sixth sentence*]. The representation of time (as ordered succession) is not given; it is generated by the intellect operating on the inner sense.

Fifth sentence [*seventh paragraph, first sentence*]. Even if my logical faculty ideally reaches beyond the sphere of human experience (§§ 21–23), and although consciousness of logical spontaneity involves consciousness of the Self, none the less I still require an organ other than that of logical spontaneity in order to know my Self or any other object. Such an organ is inner sense, upon which my spontaneity operates as productive imagination. It follows that the known Self—

composed of but not identical with my objective representations of nature—is conditioned by time, and is hence an appearance.

'in so far as I am given to myself [as something other or] beyond that [I] which is [given to myself] in intuition' —namely, as an identical Self; whereas intuition in itself is merely equivalent to the various states of my consciousness.

Last sentence. If one admits that everything spatial is merely phenomenal, one ought also to admit that the knowable Self is similarly only a phenomenon. For we have seen that the representation of ordered time depends on the movement which orders space. This movement is an action of the productive imagination. As a result, the Self which I represent as enduring is nothing other than an appearance.

KANT'S SECOND FOOTNOTE Kant is here trying to offer an account in psychological terms of his doctrine of the inner sense or of the self-affecting mind; or rather he is trying to interpret what he calls the 'act of attention' within the framework of the critical philosophy. He says: whenever we consciously attend to an impression, the understanding —which determines the inner sense—transforms successive (diverse) representations into simultaneous representations; in this way, it makes inherences as a unified whole, i.e. as substance, intelligible.

KANT'S DOCTRINE OF THE INNER SENSE AND THE SELF AS APPEARANCE

When I am conscious of my Self, I am conscious of my spontaneous faculty of apperception by means of synthesis. Apperception is thus the foundation upon which my representation of the Self is ultimately based. But self-consciousness, looked at in this way, is merely consciousness of a function; in self-consciousness I think of my Self merely as something existing, i.e. as spontaneity. But I am also in a position to intuit my Self, i.e. to represent my Self and its properties as content. The inner sense makes this possible. My Self as content (i.e. my sensible or empirical Self) consists of sensations referring to nature—more precisely, of sensations of which I am conscious, i.e. of sensations (present or not present) as representations. Accordingly, my Self as an object of intuition is the totality of my sensations transformed into a single consciousness, i.e. my determinate inner sense.

The manifold of my representations is successive; in other words, the form of inner sense is time. For this reason, the determination of inner sense occurs in time; indeed, it *is* the determination of time. Consequently, as an object capable of being intuited and conceived, viz. as something enduring whose states succeed each other, the Self is like any other object in time; it is thus an appearance. On the other hand, as noumenon the Self must be thought of as independent of time and synthetic order.

Hence the inner sense can be described both as a faculty —that of intuiting the Self—and as its own object—the Self. And although this view involves a difficulty, it is a difficulty, Kant says, 'common to every theory' (*scil.* of the Self) (B 68 and B 155).

We may also say of the mind as inner sense that it 'affects' itself (B 67 f.); for, as an organ of self-intuition, it determines the Self through the form inherent in it, time.

Thus, whereas for Locke the inner sense is an exclusively receptive organ and thus refers to the Self as its source or given object, for the critical philosophy the inner sense is a mediating organ upon which the Self depends. Indeed, we may say that the inner sense produces the Self, even if it does not do so spontaneously, for the inner sense is subordinate to the logical faculty of apperception; apperception, operating as productive imagination, generates the Self as a substance originally manifesting itself in time.

SECTION 25

Résumé

Although consciousness of my own spontaneity is consciousness of my own existence as a thinking subject, it does not involve knowledge of the true nature of my Self. For, independently of my understanding and the form of my inner sense, the Self which I represent does not exist at all. I can represent and know my Self only as something enduring through its successive states and co-existing with a multiplicity of possible representations, i.e. as phenomenon and not as thing-in-itself. Only in the case of the intuitive intellect, where the act of thought is also the act of knowing, can one assume that self-consciousness coincides with knowledge of the Self (and the whole of nature).

Explanation

This section is closely connected with the second part of § 24. Kant continues his account of his doctrine of the Self as appearance.

First sentence. All that follows from the fact of self-consciousness, i.e. consciousness of the logical faculty, is the existence of the Self as a thinking subject.

Second sentence. Self-consciousness is merely consciousness of self as logical spontaneity; it by no means involves knowledge of the nature of the Self, or its absolute properties.

Third sentence [*third and fourth sentences*]. All knowledge of the Self (as of any other object) requires a medium of intuition. Thus, although the Self of whose existence I am immediately conscious is not an appearance, the Self which I know is phenomenal—though by no means an illusion.[9]

Fourth sentence [*fifth sentence*]. It follows that our own self-consciousness is not the same as knowledge of the Self, in spite of the fact that ideally the categories are valid outside the field of our experience, i.e. in spite of the fact that ideally our self-consciousness is identical with the construction of objects.

Fifth sentence [*sixth, seventh and eighth sentences*]. Just as pure form by itself does not constitute knowledge, so also consciousness of my own spontaneity does not involve knowledge

[9] On Kant's distinction between 'appearance' and 'illusion', cf. § 8 III and the commentary thereto.

of the Self. Our knowledge does not depend exclusively on the spontaneous faculty; it requires in addition a medium of intuition. Only in the case of an intuitive understanding, which requires neither a sensible medium nor even the categories, can it be said that self-consciousness and knowledge of the Self completely coincide.

FOOTNOTE TO § 25 In this note, which falls into two parts, Kant completes his refutation of the Cartesian philosophy. In the first part of the note he merely emphasises once more that consciousness of my own spontaneity, which is consciousness of my Self as a thinking subject, is not knowledge of the Self—is not knowledge of the nature and properties of the Self.

In the second part of this footnote (beginning with the words 'Now since I do not have another') Kant adds the following reflection: although my spontaneity as such is independent of time, I am still unable to know my spontaneous Self. In order to know my spontaneous Self I would need a medium in which my Self as spontaneity could manifest itself; but such a medium is not given to me—indeed, such a medium is inconceivable.

We can only conceive of an intuitive intellect, not of our own intellect, that it should possess knowledge of its own creative power before that power is actually exercised, i.e. that it should create the universe merely by becoming conscious of its own creative power. For it can be assumed that the creative power inherent in the intuitive understanding is the Creator himself. But we are not so endowed that we create and know things merely by becoming conscious of our own spontaneous faculty. On the contrary, it is only given to us to know what we have already created, i.e. appearances.

SECTION § 26

In this section Kant completes the argument of the 'Transcendental Deduction'. He shows that the objects of our perception—and therefore the objects of our experience—are nothing other than matter ordered in space and time in accordance with the categories or the materially filled and categorically determined forms of intuition; and that, as a consequence, apprehension (our faculty of perception) and apperception (our conceptual faculty operating on matter through the media of space and time) coincide.

Thus, Kant finally proves in § 26 that the nature we know, the organised phenomenal world, is generated by our own logical spontaneity; that therefore the logical act of unifying a manifold is also a metaphysical act which creates phenomenal nature.

Also in this section Kant gives the precise limits within which the results of the 'Transcendental Deduction' are applicable. He establishes (1) that the categories are valid only for appearances; (2) that, although the categories represent the universal fundamental laws upon which the organisation of nature is based, it is not possible to derive any particular laws from the categories.

Résumé

FIRST, SECOND AND THIRD PARAGRAPHS It will now be shown, by way of conclusion, that the categories are actually valid for all the objects of our experience, i.e. for nature as we know it.

Indeterminate nature can always be described as indeterminate space–time; determinate nature (the object) can always be described as determinate space–time.

Hence, organised (determinate) nature can always be construed as space–time, materially filled and ordered by our own spontaneity.

For space and time are nothing other than a manifold of representations, referring to three-dimensional externality and given as succession. Determinate space–time coincides with our organised representations. Our organised representations, finally, are the same as our consciousness, organised in accordance with the categories as a unified manifold.

The above proof may also be stated as follows. If the mind, referring to nature as matter in space and time, is called apprehension, and the mind, referring to nature as pure space–time, is called apperception, it follows that the unity generated by the synthesis of apprehension must always correspond to the unity generated by the synthesis of apperception; that is to say, the objects of perception must always accord with the categories.

FOURTH PARAGRAPH (*Kant's first example*). To what extent is my empirical perception of a house based on the action of my spontaneous logical faculty? My determinate representation of a house, i.e. of materially filled determinate space, is originally nothing other than the representation—generated by my spontaneous faculty—of a (synthetic) unity composed of numerical unities in accordance with a principle.

For what we perceive as a house is basically the indeterminate source of our sensations (e.g. of light and shade) constructed by our understanding as a geometrical figure, i.e. as logical (synthetic) unity manifested in space.

FIFTH PARAGRAPH (*Kant's second example*). To what extent is my empirical perception of a natural event, e.g. the freezing of water, based on the action of my spontaneous faculty? A natural event may be described as two mutually exclusive states of one and the same appearance (e.g. of water turning into ice). Again, the two mutually exclusive states can be regarded as states succeeding each other in a determinate order, i.e. as two segments of time. Finally, the two segments of time may be construed as logically determinate time or as thought manifested in time.

For time is given to us as an infinite and indeterminate magnitude; by ordering time, i.e. by logically determining it, we organise nature appearing in time. Organised nature, as a chain of causes and effects, is thus nothing other than coherent thought manifested or realised in time.

SIXTH AND SEVENTH PARAGRAPHS It can thus be maintained

that the human understanding legislates for nature. It does so in the following way.

The nature we know must be regarded as a spatio-temporal appearance and not as a thing-in-itself. All connectedness in an appearance is attributed to a connecting intellect and is not to be supposed inherent in the appearance itself. Thus, nature as a connected whole is nature organised through the human understanding with the assistance of the categories.

The categories are what are called the fundamental laws of nature; all particular laws must harmonise with these basic laws. Of course, particular laws cannot be derived exclusively from the categories; on the contrary, in so far as they do not follow analytically from the fundamental laws they must be individually discovered by observing appearances and the changes of appearances.

Explanation

FIRST PARAGRAPH In the 'Metaphysical Deduction' Kant derived the pure forms or categories as such, i.e. as the determinate and basic forms of logical unity; in the preceding part of the 'Transcendental Deduction' he shows that the categories, as the forms of logical unity, are ideally valid for any given manifold. In the present section § 26, Kant finally proves that the categories do actually determine *our* experience; that the structure of all the objects of our perception is in accordance with the categories; in short, that what we call laws of nature are nothing other than applied categories.

SECOND PARAGRAPH Kant here introduces the terms 'apprehension' and 'synthesis of apprehension'. Whereas apperception is the faculty of thinking the unified manifold, apprehension is our faculty of perceiving natural unities, i.e. objects. Assuming that nothing is given apart from spatio–temporally bound matter, i.e. sensations as indeterminate representations, it follows that apprehension is our faculty of transforming an indeterminate manifold of representations (matter) into unified determinate representations (natural unities or objects). Such a transformation is an act of synthesis.

In short: apperception unifies any given nature understood as a mere manifold of representations. Given nature, understood as a manifold of representations referring to filled space–time, is synthetically produced by apprehension. (Cf. commentary to paragraph 3, sentence 3, of the present section; also the résumé.)

THIRD PARAGRAPH *First sentence.* Space and time are given to us as the forms of intuition. The synthetic act of apprehension must always accord with these forms of intuition. That is to say: the representations resulting from this synthesis must always refer to a three-dimensional externality, and its object must always be in time. In short: nature, which underlies apprehension, is indeterminate space–time.

Second sentence. Space and time are also given to us as intuitions. Whatever is given to us can always be described as determinate space and time—this is also true of nature grasped in apprehension. (On space and time as forms of intuition and as pure intuition, cf. commentary to § 1; also commentary to §§ 2, 4, 6.)

Third sentence. Since space and time are given to us as indeterminate magnitudes and since spontaneity is responsible for all determination, there is an indissoluble connection between the determination of perceptible nature and that of space and time. That is to say: in unifying matter, apprehension also unifies space and time; more precisely: the mind, in forming matter, as apprehension, as apperception forms time and space.

'The unity of the synthesis of the manifold': the highest unity implying connection. Kant, in the introductory § 15, describes the investigation of this unity as the peculiar task of the critical philosophy. He explains here that this unity is already given to us as (determinate) space outside us or as (determinate) time within us.

KANT'S THEORETICAL PHILOSOPHY

'given—not indeed in, but with these intuitions': although the intuitions of space and time are given to us simultaneously with synthetic unity, i.e. are given to us synthetically united, none the less the unity in question does not arise in space and time but within our own spontaneous faculty.

Fourth sentence. Space and time are nothing but a succession of representations referring to a three-dimensional externality. Unified space and time coincide with the representation of something enduring whose parts are co-existent and simultaneous but whose states are mutually exclusive, i.e. necessarily successive. Unified space–time is thus nothing other than the unified manifold, or the categories applied to space and time. For the representation of unified space–time is the representation of an object in general as a numerical unity (quantity); as something real (quality); as something composed of inherences (substance); as something changing (relation). Unified space–time is also the same as our own organised consciousness, emerging from an indeterminate manifold of representations as a determinate representation.

Fifth sentence. Finally, it follows from what has been said that the categories determine all the objects of our perception and thus of our experience too—for experience is knowledge based on perception.

KANT'S FIRST FOOTNOTE This footnote has already been discussed above (cf. the relation of the 'Transcendental Analytic' to the 'Transcendental Aesthetic', pp. 74 f.); it has also been partially explained in the commentary to § 24, to which Kant makes reference at the end of this note (cf. pp. 180 f.). All that needs to be added here is this: in order to strengthen and explain the argument of the main text, Kant argues that space and time cannot be represented as merely indeterminate magnitudes; on the contrary, it is the synthetic acts of the understanding which first make possible the representations of space and time. That is to say: if space and time are given to us as the modes of our receptivity, the unified representations of space and time involve determination; this determination depends on the unifying acts of our spontaneous understanding.

'Form of intuition': intuition *as* form; potentially determining; merely given nature as a succession of representations referring to infinite space.

'Formal intuition': intuition *of the* form; space and time as determinate. Represented nature as enduring three-dimensional unity.[10]

FOURTH PARAGRAPH Kant illustrates his proof by means of two examples. The first is intended to make clear the validity of the category of quantity; the second to show the validity of the category of causality for all empirical perception. The two examples are implicitly designed to show the validity of *all* the categories for our experience.

As we have already explained, in the critical philosophy the empirical manifold is matter understood as a manifold of sensations—sensations through which matter in us reacts to the matter outside us (cf. § 3, paragraph 8). The empirical view[11] is that our perception, e.g. of a house, is based on our sensations, e.g. of colour, light and shade. This view deeply influenced Kant. He takes it as his foundation, develops it and maintains that although sensations are the empirical basis of our perception (say, of a house), the unitary and conscious perception—or 'picture'—of the house is generated by a spontaneous act of our understanding. It is through the understanding, namely, that we transform the indeterminate source of our sensations into a geometrical figure, i.e. into a system of logical relations manifested in space.

---

[10] The expression 'formal intuition' occurs for the first time in the second edition; cf. also Vleeschauwer *L'Evolution de la pensée Kantienne*, Paris, 1939, pp. 119 f. Vleeschauwer, unlike Vaihinger, tries to make plain the *unity* of the development of Kant's thought; he rightly adds here that Kant's concept of 'formal intuition', though developed later, in no way contradicts the doctrine of the first edition.

[11] According to Hume's theory of substance.

KANT'S THEORETICAL PHILOSOPHY

Here follows an account of the argument which the first example is intended to illustrate.

X—say, a house—is given to me as many different representations (sensations, e.g. light and shade). Such an X can be regarded as matter filling indeterminate space or as indeterminate space materially filled.

Apprehension, in transforming my various representations into a unity within space, generates determinate space (an object, e.g. a house). But this unity is none other than that involved in the category of quantity. For if we disregard the fact that our representations are given to us as diverse sensations, i.e. as sensations referring to space; and if we assume that our representations are presented to us as a mere manifold of representations, we may conclude that our spontaneity—transcendentally construed—transforms such a manifold into a pure (synthetic) numerical unity. This again is logical unity. It is nothing other than the unity constructed out of unities in accordance with a principle; i.e. it is numerical unity understood as a compound whole or as a system of relations, and thus an archetypal form of thought, i.e. the category of quantity (cf. commentary to § 10).

Textual. 'Apprehension' seems better, since it is more in keeping with the context. (Cf. Kant's second footnote to § 26.) 'Apperception', which appears from the fourth edition onwards, is of course 'empirical apperception' (apprehension); cf. commentary to § 16, paragraph 1, sentence 5.

SECOND FOOTNOTE TO § 26 Kant here explains the principle of the argument which the two examples are intended to illustrate. The intention is to show that the unity generated by the synthesis of apprehension is always the same as that generated by the synthesis of apperception.

'Imagination', here contrasted with the understanding as a purely intellectual faculty (cf. §§ 23 and 24), includes both the transcendental productive imagination and the empirical imagination which manifests itself in the synthesis of apprehension.

KANT'S THEORY OF INHERENCE AND SUBSTANCE

What is the 'nature', the 'substance' of this unique object before me? According to Kant, although this 'nature' is unique it is not originally one. It—or the object—must rather be described as a combination of many elements or as a compound whole whose uniqueness is based on the totality of its content. Thus, for example, the uniqueness of the carnation I see before me consists of a multiplicity of elements which together produce a unitary structure.

And yet when I grasp 'carnation' I am not immediately conscious of all the elements which together compose the carnation; nor do any of these elements belong exclusively to the carnation. How is it, then, that I am able to represent something which is infinitely various in itself and infinitely connected with other unique objects, as a finite unity—a finite unity which I can conceive as such but which I can never exhaustively describe through its content.

It is possible because the matter given to me is determined by my logical faculty through the media of intuition —and primarily that of time. The (paradoxical) concept of finite unity consisting of an infinite number of different elements and yet grasped as unity even before its elements are grasped, is explained by the fact that the unity in question is a product of my own peculiarly active faculty of representation and knowledge. This faculty is capable of pre-intuiting, as it were, the unique whole, and it can do so because it is capable of intuiting infinitely many representations (sensations) as co-existing in one time. Thus the mind, which intuits many representations variously succeeding each other as a simultaneously enduring representation, generates the picture of something unitary or of a compound whole.

The spontaneously generated representation of one (synthetic) time composed of an infinite number of simultaneous representations turns out in the end to be a logical representation. It coincides with many diverse representations thought of as *one* representation, i.e. it coincides with the representation of what can be variously though coherently described. The mind, therefore, confronted with an infinite manifold of representations, originally generates the *concept* of the unitary whole composed of such diversity, i.e. the mind generates, for example, substance composed of its inherences (*in abstracto*, without representing it). It is in this way, then, that the mind, affected by many different sensations, is able to grasp the source of those sensations—'carnation'—as a unitary spatio–temporal whole, i.e. as the 'substance' of the various sensations (*in concreto*).

Such a representation of a unitary whole consisting of a manifold of representations is the foundation of the (general) concept implying other concepts, and therefore also of all natural knowledge. For (1) a unitary representation may be conceived as infinitely applicable in its entirety (i.e. as generic concept, e.g. of carnation, applying to its objects through the mediation of a schema—cf. A 141/B 180); (2) a unitary representation may be conceived under any of the elements contained in it, i.e. as abstraction, e.g. 'redness' and therefore as inherence, i.e. as a constituent part of many objects yet to be known. (In this connection cf. 'Kant's reform of logic' I, particularly pp. 21 f., and also the commentary to Kant's footnote, § 16.)

In this way, by acts of conception and judgement, the human mind is able to acquire clear knowledge of the nature which it creates itself. For the unique objects of which it is conscious are the products of its own logical faculty—a faculty which universally and necessarily organises the matter given to it through the senses and through the mediating forms of space and time inherent in itself.

KANT'S THEORY OF CAUSALITY

Kant's second example is intended to show how the category of causality underlies all our perception of natural events and thus our experience and knowledge of nature.

Kant's doctrine of causality is one of his most important and influential achievements. An account of this doctrine is given not only here in the 'Transcendental Deduction' but also in a chapter devoted especially to the topic, under the title 'Second analogy'. I think, however, that a careful interpretation of the present section will suffice for a full understanding of Kant's doctrine of causality.

Let us begin by comparing the critical doctrine of causality with the empirical and sceptical theories. What we naïvely take to be the real states of a real thing changing under the influence of a cause; what we sceptically regard as merely temporally connected representations or as constantly conjoined impressions of natural events, turns out, in the critical investigation, to be the category of causality manifested in time, and ultimately to be the principle of synthetic unity, i.e. logical consistency of thought universally applied to nature as a principle of all change.

What we naïvely regard as the states of a thing is, in the critical philosophy, nothing other than two necessarily successive periods of time. And what we call an instance of causality is always an appearance presented in two successive states, i.e. the category of causality realised in the phenomenal world.

In order to understand Kant's doctrine it is necessary above all to realise that any event can be construed as change, and that any change can be construed as two successive states of one and the same appearance; and in saying this, the cause is always thought of as being contained in the succession of the two states. For example, if the two states are water and ice, and the event—or change—the water's freezing, we can describe the succession of events as 'water under the influence of cold ($=$ ice)'. The representation of the two states includes the concept of cause. But which is the cause, in any given case, is something which can be decided only by empirical investigation. (Indeed, in any given case it is quite possible that many causes may be found for a single event; science will then, for its own reasons, emphasise one or the other.)

Besides, as Kant explains in the 'Second analogy' (A 202 f./B 247 f.) by the example of a stove heating a room, cause and effect may at times be simultaneous; yet we must always regard the cause as preceding the effect. Again, it is possible that our representations of an unchanging object, such as a house, in ranging from one part of the object to another, may well be empirically successive. And yet we take the roof of a house to be necessarily simultaneous with its walls. Such empirical and psychological observations can be transcendentally explained as follows: time is given to us indeterminately; by logically determining time through the category of causality, we ourselves transform time into a series of necessarily successive periods (and afterwards we can then represent them subjectively as simultaneous; cf. § 18).

Although Kant's theory of causality is based on that of Hume (who deeply influenced him) it is the exact opposite of Hume's conception. Hume maintains that what we regard as causal connection is in fact merely temporal connection, i.e. the association of two impressions immediately succeeding each other. Kant maintains that what gives us the impression of temporal connection is in fact the category of causality confronting us in time as necessary succession.

By reversing Hume's theory of causality and substituting a constructive philosophy for Hume's penetrating scepticism, Kant succeeded in convincingly reasserting the dominion of thought over given nature. For, according to Kant, mathematics and physics are logic realised in space and time; the organisation of nature thus turns out to be a product of the human understanding. But he also maintained that a logic realised neither as mathematics in space nor as space and time in physics, was empty and futile. Kant thus not only discredited a certain kind of ontological–metaphysical thought; he also discredited all speculative thought whatever and raised science to the throne of philosophy.[12]

[12] All I mean is that this has been the historical impact of Kant's philosophy, as far as we can judge today. Kant's achievement represents

TRANSCENDENTAL DEDUCTION

SUMMARY OF KANT'S THEORY OF CAUSALITY It is assumed that nothing is given to us except a succession of representations (manifold of sensations referring to indeterminate space), i.e. matter filling indeterminate space–time. We have seen how our understanding, assisted by productive imagination, transforms such a manifold of sensations into the determinate representation of an appearance (cf. commentary to § 26, paragraph 4). What has now to be made clear is how our spontaneity transforms such a manifold into the representation of an appearance constantly changing in accordance with a principle, i.e. into nature constantly changing in accordance with the law of cause and effect.

My spontaneity, operating on the succession of my representations (indeterminate time), is able to generate the determinate picture of time as something enduring through successive and mutually exclusive phases. Now, what strikes us as the successive states of one and the same appearance is nothing other than materially filled time. For time is not given to us as empty time; it is rather present before me as a manifold of representations referring to materially filled, three-dimensional space. Thus, in generating the picture of determinate time, my spontaneity orders my representations, i.e. organises the matter before my senses as an enduring (spatial) entity whose states or phenomenal forms necessarily succeed each other in determinate order.

The principle my spontaneity thus imposes on time is logical in character. It is nothing other than the principle of logically consistent thought in general. It is in accordance with this principle that I determine a given entity in itself, and I do so by construing it as a compound and deriving its elements from each other. The enduring entity, appearing in time and manifesting itself in necessarily successive periods of time, is thus ultimately nature construed as

---

the best proof of the incomparable originality of genuine philosophy not only influencing the progress of science but also guiding and inspiring every kind of creative activity.

something identical, determinate in itself and within which B depends on A, C on B, and so on.

It can thus be maintained that even our perception of natural events depends on logical spontaneity. For what we perceive as an event (change), is time ordered as two periods of time; or: the indeterminate source of my representations (various sensations) construed as two states of the same appearance. In this way, my spontaneity, by logically ordering the given manifold, metaphysically generates the appearance of nature constantly changing in accordance with a law.

SECTION 26 (*continued*)

FIFTH PARAGRAPH (KANT'S SECOND EXAMPLE) *First sentence.* When I perceive a natural event, e.g. water freezing, I represent the same entity twice, i.e. in two successive states (water and ice).

Second sentence. But an identical appearance is time, materially filled and synthetically unified. Thus the principle of synthetic unity, appearing in time as something both enduring and *passing successively through different phases*, also involves a law regulating events.

Third sentence. But this law as such, i.e. as the logical principle of the necessary succession or derivability of one thing from another, applied to nature (materially filled time), is the category of causality. It is this alone which enables me to construe the whole of nature as an uninterrupted chain of causes and effects.

Fourth sentence. Thus what I have called a causally determined event ultimately depends on the act of my logical spontaneity operating on materially filled time, i.e. phenomenal nature. Indeed, I should not even be able to perceive an event if the principle of causality were not inherent in me, for it is this principle which enables me to construe two phenomena (water and ice) as two necessarily and universally connected states of the same appearance.

SIXTH AND SEVENTH PARAGRAPHS Kant here formulates the

surprising and sensational conclusion of the critical investigation: the human understanding itself legislates for nature through the categories. He then goes on to summarise the argument of the 'Transcendental Deduction' (cf. résumé). Bodies in space, objects composed of properties, natural events—these are perceptible only through the categories of quantity, substance and causality respectively.

The categories are the universal laws upon which nature as a connected whole depends. Our knowledge, however, includes many particular laws referring to particular connections within the general system of nature. Such particular connections are non-necessary, i.e. statements referring to them could quite well turn out to be mistaken. It is thus possible, for example, that a particular law, based on wide experience and frequent observation, should for a long while constitute an important part of our view of nature. But it is conceivable that, at a later date, a new (particular) law should be discovered which conflicted with and thus invalidated the earlier knowledge. None the less, according to Kant, the categories must always be the foundation of research and knowledge, irrespective of all the possible discoveries which may be made in the future.

SECTION 27

Introductory

Kant now explains (1) that only when applied to the matter of our experience do the categories lead to knowledge; (2) that the categories determine our experience; (3) that the categories—valid not only for the human intellect but for any non-divine intellect whatever—are the objective forms of pure logic; they are by no means accidentally innate in the human mind.

Résumé

Although the categories are pure logical forms, i.e. are present *a priori*, in themselves they contain no *a priori* knowledge. For whatever *a priori* knowledge we are able to acquire arises from the application of the categories to the matter of our experience, i.e. to indeterminate (materially filled) space–time.

But since it would be absurd to suppose that the laws of logic are inherent in (the matter of) experience, it follows that any empirical philosophy or any kind of psychological interpretation of our knowledge of nature would be insufficient and unsatisfactory. For any theory disputing the logical character of nature's organisation deprives it of its necessary character and is thus merely scepticism.

Explanation

FIRST PARAGRAPH In the earlier parts of the 'Deduction' Kant emphasises that, ideally, the categories were valid outside the sphere of human experience; he now emphasises that the categories are actually limited to the objects of our experience.

First sentence. Any object, thought or known by us, coincides with a category manifested in time and space.

Second sentence. Any object known by us presupposes matter. That is to say: any object known by us is simply space–time organised in accordance with the categories and materially filled, or matter (the source of our sensations) constructed as an object in space and time in accordance with the categories.

Third sentence. All knowledge based on matter (sensations) is called 'experience'.

Fourth sentence. Hence *a priori* knowledge, based on the application of the pure forms to matter (indeterminate space–time), is possible only in combination with experience. That is to say: knowledge, even if it can be called *a priori*, arises from the application of the categories, not to the pure, but to the materially filled forms of intuition.

KANT'S FOOTNOTE This footnote is obviously intended to prepare the reader for an understanding of the *Critique of Practical Reason*. In this work Kant maintains the view that reason applies the category of causality to the human will, by means of the moral law; and that the category thus has a fruitful use independently of matter, not indeed in a theoretical sense but in a practical sense. (cf. *Critique of Practical Reason*, 'On the deduction of the principles of practical reason').

The rest of § 27

In the remaining part of § 27 Kant shows that neither empiricism nor what one might call 'transcendental subjectivism' is capable of explaining the organisation of nature in terms of a necessarily valid law.

SECOND PARAGRAPH Since the laws of logic cannot possibly originate in experience and since the nature we know is logically organised, we can only draw the conclusion that logic, by its laws, i.e. our own spontaneous conceptual faculty, determines nature.[13]

THIRD PARAGRAPH Kant here gives an outline of what one might call 'transcendental psychology' (or 'transcendental subjectivism'). It is possible that Kant was thinking of one of his contemporary critics—or misinterpreters—who, by combining transcendental and Leibnizian concepts, attempted to refute the critical philosophy and replace it with a variation of Hume's scepticism. According to such a philosophy, as outlined here by Kant, nature would indeed conform to the categories; these categories, however, would not be pure logical rules but merely subjective dispositions implanted in us by God who would have so organised nature that it accorded with our subjective mental dispositions.

Kant argues that it would be inappropriate to appeal to God in support of such a hypothesis. If we make God the

[13] For a precise explanation of the biological analogies ('epigenesis' and 'pre-formation system of pure reason') by means of which Kant sought to clarify the difference between his own and other possible theories, cf. H. Paton, *Kant's Metaphysic of Experience*, London, 1936, vol. I, p. 578, and also A. C. Ewing, *A short commentary to Kant's 'Critique of Pure Reason'*, London, 1938, p. 130.

source of the merely accidental, psychological dispositions or forms of thought with which nature had miraculously to conform, we turn all our knowledge into illusion. It is also obvious that any theory can be justified on the assumption of divine intervention. But above all, as soon as we replace logic by psychology we destroy the concept of necessity which logic, and logic alone, possesses and thus we destroy the very foundation of all fruitful philosophy whatever. For if we assume that nature is organised in accordance with, not logical, but merely psychological—and by a miracle—necessary laws, we make any genuinely constructive philosophy impossible; we would inevitably fall a prey either to sophistical dogmatism or sceptical chaos.

KANT'S SYNOPSIS OF THE 'TRANSCENDENTAL DEDUCTION'

Kant's 'synopsis' consists of three observations or, rather, definitions.

He explains that in the 'Deduction' he has shown the following:

1. The categories and hence all our *a priori* theoretical knowledge (consisting of synthetic *a priori* judgements) are the principles of the nature we are able to experience; i.e. that they are the basic rules in accordance with which spatio–temporally bound matter is organised.
2. The materially filled forms of spatio–temporal intuition are determined by these basic rules.
3. Such determination is ultimately the organisation of our own consciousness (i.e. the organisation of a succession of representations referring to indeterminate space) into a unified manifold. That is to say: determination is spontaneously realised by my own logical faculty imprinting its categorical form on primary matter, viz. on the original intuitions of space and time; these latter are a succession of representations referring to indeterminate (materially filled) space, i.e. the two forms originally attaching to my sensibility.

PHENOMENA AND NOUMENA
(A 235–A 260/B 294–B 315)

Kant's unified theory of the thing-in-itself

I

As Kant himself says, the chapter on phenomena and noumena has no new conclusions to offer. And yet a special value attaches to this section, in which Kant presents a more detailed,[1] though not always a more explicit,[2] account of the doctrine of the thing-in-itself than he does elsewhere in the *Critique of Pure Reason*. For, as Kant himself suggests, the concept of the thing-in-itself contains the critical philosophy *in nuce*. Thus in seeking to understand his doctrine of the thing-in-itself we are also attempting to understand both the metaphysical and logical aspects of Kant's philosophy, i.e. to understand the new relation of thought and reality, the new unity of logic and metaphysics brought about by Kant. This, in my opinion, was his principal and most influential achievement.

And yet it is precisely this section—or the question it discusses—which has been characterised as the 'seed-bed of all the contradictions discovered in the *Critique of Pure Reason*' (Windelband).[3] In particular, Kant's distinction between the negative and the positive noumenon is supposed to betray two contradictory tendencies in his thought. For example, the above distinction is supposed to reveal a divergence between the final conclusions of his theoretical philosophy and those of his practical philosophy; or between his mature critical view and a pre-critical position which he never completely abandoned and which is often described as 'naïve Realism'.

[1] § 23 ends with a reference to the more detailed account in this chapter.
[2] Cf. below, p. 207, footnote 5.
[3] Following Schopenhauer's example; cf. 'Introduction'.

KANT'S THEORETICAL PHILOSOPHY

But I hope to be able to show that there is no contradiction nor even the slightest inconsistency either within the section itself, or between it and any other section in the *Critique*, or finally between the first and second editions of this chapter. While it is true that the two editions differ from each other, the difference is not one of content revealing various phases in Kant's philosophical development; it is one of improved terminology and heightened clarity of presentation.

Let us begin by summarising the argument of the chapter.

Since the value of any philosophical theory consists in its capacity to serve as a guide-line to human work and endeavour; and since the value of the critical philosophy in particular consists in its establishing the limits within which human enquiry may successfully be pursued and beyond which human knowledge can never hope to penetrate, it follows that, since the concept of the thing-in-itself is a limiting concept, its full elucidation must be a worthwhile and profitable undertaking.

It has been shown (throughout the first part of the *Critique of Pure Reason*) that the categories lead to knowledge only when applied to space and time (nature), but that divorced from the form of inner sense, time, they are empty. It follows that mere thought does not establish reality; indeed, it establishes nothing at all. Thus mere thought or that which is merely thought—the noumenon—has only a negative significance. Were there a kind of thought which actually established reality, it would be totally different from our own kind of thought. Assuming that such thought were possible, we could characterise the object of its thought as the positive noumenon. But we know nothing about such positive noumenon nor about such thought. As a result, the concept of the negative noumenon—i.e. the representation of our thought not applied to humanly possible experience—is, to put it precisely, a limiting concept.[4]

---

[4] Or: the distinction between the positive and negative noumenon becomes meaningless when the noumenon is regarded as a limiting con-

The above argument may be briefly summarised as follows. Logic, which is our kind of thought, cannot produce knowledge of true Being or of absolute reality. Thought corresponding to true Being is altogether beyond our powers of comprehension.[5]

Only by distinguishing true Being from knowable reality was Kant able to set up a logic of construction; only by construing the universe in two senses, viz. as appearance and as thing-in-itself (B XXVII), was he able to reform traditional logic. Only by completely separating the concept of true Being from that of phenomenal reality can we prevent thought—trapped in a constant vicious circle— from proceeding analytically from concept to reality and from reality to concept; i.e. only by making this sharp distinction shall we prevent thought from degenerating into mere tautology and from leading inevitably to scepticism or arbitrary and deceptive construction.

The logical significance of Kant's distinction between phenomena and noumena may also be explained as follows:

1. Logic is described as the art of connective thought and

---

cept. As is generally known, Kant does not oppose the positive to the negative noumenon in the first edition (cf. below, p. 212). But in one passage common to both editions (A 255/B 311) Kant speaks of the 'merely negative use of the noumenon' (irrespective of whether the noumenon is positive or negative). That is to say, as a limiting concept the noumenon is identical.

[5] In a sense, Kant's account of the thing-in-itself in §§ 21–23 is more explicit than that in the present section. Here Kant compares only two possible kinds of categorical thought with intellectual intuition: (1) their application to spatio-temporally bound matter (2) their purely intellectual use. In the 'Deduction,' however, in addition to discussing the purely intellectual use of the category (§ 22), Kant also expressly discusses their possible application to pure space–time (§ 22) and their application to an intuition other than our own (§ 23). By adopting these two latter points of view he not only makes the concept of the negative noumenon fully explicit; but their adoption enables him to give an exhaustive account of the critical theory of the universal validity of logic (of which only the Creator has no need). The present section scarcely refers to these two viewpoints: A 254/B 309.

nature as a complex phenomenon whose organisation is connectedness. Unless we are willing to suppose that—by a miracle, as it were—thoughts are connected in precisely the same way in which natural appearances are interconnected, we must construe our connective acts of thought as acts of valid construction, i.e. as acts through which we construct or generate nature as a connected phenomenon (synthetic unity). The phenomenal world is thus understood as synthetic unity produced by the application of our thought to the media given with our senses. True Being, on the other hand, not arising from connective thought, is an absolute unity. But for us both absolute unity and non-connective thought are quite unknowable and inconceivable.

Our kind of thought consists in distinguishing, comparing and equating, and the unity which we can produce by thought is only synthetic or phenomenal unity—a unity which is also diversity, an eternal paradox. It is, however, conceivable that there is another kind of unity, which is absolute and non-paradoxical. But an intellect not needing logic, not needing to distinguish, compare or equate in order to think or know is for ever beyond our powers of comprehension.

2. Nature may be described from two points of view: as indeterminate or determinate. Indeterminate nature is nature which we cannot experience, conceive or know; determinate nature is nature experienced, conceived and known. The thing-in-itself, neither knowable nor thinkable nor capable of being experienced by us, is for us absolutely indeterminate; but it is conceivable that for the divine intellect it is absolutely determinate.[6]

[6] It may be added that for reason, i.e. in the pure logical sense, the thing-in-itself is determinate; cf. the section 'On the transcendental ideal': 'the concept of a thing . . . is completely determined in and through itself' (A 576/B 604) and that by excluding all predicates not attaching to being. But to think an object and to know it are two different things: such a completely determinate concept of pure reason contains no knowledge. As far as this is concerned, i.e. for the under-

3. Finally, the world of our experience may also be represented from the form–matter point of view. Indeterminate nature is mere matter and non-determinative thought is mere form. Within determinate nature—i.e. in nature experienced, conceived and known by us—form and matter, though distinguishable, are indissolubly bound up with each other. We can thus characterise determinate nature as matter formed, and determinative thought we can characterise as form forming matter. And whereas the world we know contains both form and matter, and whereas we can neither conceive mere form nor perceive mere matter, the thing-in-itself is thought of as being independent of both form and matter. It is conceivable that the divine intellect, but not our own, creates (thinks and knows) matter by creating form, and generates form by generating matter. Thus even the distinction between form and matter, for so long regarded as the most profound and most significant distinction of all, loses both its meaning and its epistemological value when applied to the thing-in-itself.

Thought can be conceived as valid, constructive, systematic and necessary only if true Being is made completely independent of both matter and form, only if phenomenal reality is construed as the product of the spontaneous forms operating on given nature matter.

That is the logical significance of Kant's doctrine of the thing-in-itself. Its metaphysical significance is this:

Unless we assume that our constructive thought refers exclusively to phenomenal reality, we deny all reality; and in denying all reality, whether it be called God or the noumenon, we are behaving absurdly. For we therewith destroy the whole foundation not only of all thought but of all human endeavour whatever. And yet we may not assume that we can know the thing-in-itself through phenomena, or phenomena through the thing-in-itself.[7] For although all phenomena, inclusive of ourselves, depend on

---

standing, the thing-in-itself remains something merely negative or indeterminable.   [7] Similarly A. C. Ewing, loc. cit., p. 194.

an absolute source of reality,[8] none the less our knowledge of phenomena (whether of nature or of the Self) is totally independent of the thing-in-itself. In short: the thing-in-itself is absolute reality; but absolute reality is completely divorced from phenomenal reality.

The concepts of the positive and negative noumenon, which are involved in Kant's doctrine of the thing-in-itself, are in no way contradictory but both turn out to be indispensable. The conception of the negative noumenon implies that thought, when not applied to the media given to us, is not an instrument of valid construction, and consequently that the phenomenal reality which we are able to experience can only be constructed by our kind of thought, i.e. by logic. (In this way knowledge is secured against the anarchy of scepticism.)

The conception of the positive noumenon involves conceding that we can never know true Being and thus we exclude it from all our enquiries. (In this way knowledge is secured against the tyranny of deceptive metaphysics.)

The thing-in-itself, as the divine source of all that exists, is absolutely real. The thing-in-itself, as something really *existent*, would be the object of divine thought, totally differing from all the objects of human thought.

The concept of the negative noumenon does not exclude the doctrine of the absolute reality of the thing-in-itself; the concept of the positive noumenon, on the other hand, does not involve the certain assertion of the actual existence of a particular thing-in-itself.

Let us now sum up what we have said so far:

1. Kant's philosophy is based metaphysically on the concept of absolute reality.

[8] It is probably this thought of Kant's which is the foundation of Windelband's famous objection that Kant applied the categories of existence, substance and causality to the thing-in-itself and its relation to phenomena and that in doing so he contradicted his own critical theory. In fact Kant succeeds in construing not only the thing-in-itself, the noumenon, but also the relation of absolute reality to phenomena as something merely negative—i.e. succeeds in holding them free from any (categorical) determination.

2. We cannot know what kind of reality this is—whether something created, or the Creator himself, or creative thought (divine spontaneity). All our concepts, analogies and descriptions turn out to be totally inefficacious and inadequate with reference to the thing-in-itself.
3. Although absolute reality is the ultimate source and foundation of all phenomena and all thought, there is no connection, knowable by us, between the unknown absolute on the one hand, and our own world of various though unified phenomena, or our differentiating and unifying thought, on the other.

II

It is obvious that Kant's doctrine of the thing-in-itself is relevant both to the philosophy of religion and to moral philosophy.

The problem of the special existence of the thing-in-itself (which Kant makes no attempt to solve) is the problem of divine existence. It is the problem, namely, of whether there is a God in the Judaeo–Christian sense of the word, as a creator standing outside and over and above his own creation; or whether there is a God in Spinoza's pantheistic sense, identical with the universe; or whether, finally, God is manifested in some medium or form unknown and inconceivable to us (language is inadequate to express this idea).

The doctrine of the *practical* reality of the thing-in-itself, however, signifies that Kant affirmed the divine nature of the moral law. This moral law—whether God be regarded as its source or as manifested in it—exists as a divine element in human nature. Thus, whereas our theoretical knowledge will always be bound to matter and will always be necessarily progressive and fragmentary, our practical knowledge, our certainty of the moral law, is for all time our inviolable heritage, to which nothing can be added and from which nothing can be taken away. And thus, although revealed religion can tell us nothing about the original act of creation nor about the nature of things, the moral law, proclaimed by revealed religion, turns out to be valid, indeed divine. Just as the faithful fulfilment of the moral law furthers belief and is itself furthered by belief, so also the connection of religion and morality is proved, to the critical understanding, to be ultimate and necessary.

In short, the thing-in-itself, i.e. divine spontaneity, in so far as it is known and revealed, is the divine will in man, the moral law.[9]

III

Let us now turn to a closer investigation of the difference between the two versions of this chapter—a difference which, as we have already said above, is exclusively one of presentation and terminology.

The chief alteration Kant made is this: in the first edition he distinguishes between the concepts 'transcendental object' and the 'noumenon as true object' (A 252); in the second edition he drops these two terms and speaks instead of the 'negative' and 'positive' noumenon.

The two terms suppressed in the second edition are obviously unsatisfactory. The term, 'true object', being itself problematic, requires further explanation, while the term 'transcendental object' (referring in the first edition to the negative noumenon) tends to obscure the difference between the negative and the positive noumenon, for the latter is also an object (namely, of divine thought). As a result, Kant eliminates the term 'transcendental object' wherever he is concerned with the difference between the positive and the negative noumenon; where this distinction appears irrelevant he retains the term 'transcendental object'. (Cf. commentary to the 'Transcendental Aesthetic', § 8 I, paragraph 5.)

Let us now turn to a second divergence between the two editions, namely, the omission in the second edition of

[9] Cf. also the 'Synopsis', p. 224 f.

certain connected paragraphs (A 241 f. and A 244 f.), where a contradiction has supposedly been discovered between the present chapter and § 10. In § 10 Kant says: 'In this treatise, I purposely omit the definitions of the categories, although I may be in possession of them' (A 82/B 108). In the first edition of the chapter 'Phenomena and Noumena' we read, however, 'But we now perceive that the ground . . .' (viz. for the fact that the categories are not defined in § 10) 'lies still deeper. We realise that we are unable to define them even if we wished' (viz. the categories *per se* cannot be grasped by us). (Cf. commentary to § 23, paragraph 1.) There then follows a long and penetrating explanation; this explanation is further illuminated by a footnote intended to show that the two assertions just quoted do not in fact conflict with each other (A 242 ff.). However, even after a close study of all Kant's supplementary explanations, one cannot escape the impression that his account is not quite satisfactory—indeed, one is tempted to conclude that Kant himself was perhaps not entirely clear in his own mind as to whether the categories were definable or not.

However, his difficulty or dilemma consisted merely in the fact that the categories—as already remarked in the first edition (A 244–245/B 302)—while not in themselves definable, are schematically definable, i.e. as temporal determinations. At first Kant was obviously unsure whether to regard a schematic definition as admissible or not; hence his feeling that it was necessary to limit what had been said in § 10. But once he had overcome his reservations the necessity disappeared and the qualifying remarks of the two paragraphs A 241 f. and A 244 f. became superfluous. There is thus no contradiction within the earlier version, nor any divergence in content between the earlier and later versions. Only the presentation has changed: it has become clearer and more direct.

The two examples just given show clearly how carefully Kant prepared the second edition and, in particular, how he strove to free the presentation and terminology from even the appearance of inconsistency. Kant, probably conscious of the effort expended in revising the *Critique of Pure Reason* for the second edition, repeats in the Preface to that edition that his work is a thoroughly unitary and consistent whole. I know of no one in the whole history of literature able to make such a claim with greater justice.

SYNOPSIS OF KANT'S THEORETICAL PHILOSOPHY

I

The spirit of the eighteenth century is manifest in the philosophical revolution initiated by Kant. The eighteenth century was an age which thought it possible to throw off the fetters of dogmatism, of traditional belief and imposed law. It was an age imbued with a high concept of humanity and by a belief in man's inherent divinity. Kant was the greatest of philosophers inspired with these ideals. He regarded it as his task to convert metaphysics into a theory of man's creative power. He hoped to achieve this end by showing that it is not necessary to make assumptions about the nature of the divine in order to explain the nature of our world; that it is not a transcendent *eidos* or prime mover but rather man's own conceptual faculty which, by giving form to matter, creates phenomenal nature; that the universe revolves around the light or sun of the human intellect, albeit a light bound to matter and incapable of shining without it: only the moral will, not the understanding of man, is free from the bondage of matter.

To show the validity of such a view, Kant was obliged to evolve a theory or hypothesis which was consistent, comprehensive and throughout applicable to nature, its object.

His hypothesis or intellectual experiment is based on the concept of synthetic unity, or synthesis; by means of this concept he seeks to embrace the whole sphere of human knowledge, *a priori* and *a posteriori*. Kant himself compares his experiment with those of the scientist and, in particular, with those of the chemist. In a chemical bond two or more elements are synthesised; in the same way, many different 'elements' are transformed by the human understanding into the appearance of nature, capable of being intuited, perceived and conceived by us. Thus Kant's intention is to develop a theory according to which each particular natural phenomenon can be construed as synthetic unity within the comprehensive synthetic unity of nature as a whole; the act of synthesis itself is to be construed as a logical act of the understanding. That is to say: it is not only appearances but also concepts and judgements which are to be interpreted as unities produced by synthesis.

If we assume that there is, on the one hand, an objective nature immutably following necessary laws, and, on the other, the human mind, whose faculty of representation is spontaneous and creative, the chief problem is to show how the logical synthetic act can be formative or objectively legislative; i.e. how logical relations—and this is the metaphysical side of Kant's work—are transformed into what one might call phenomenal reality.

The ultimate medium (including space and time) through which this becomes possible is the human consciousness. The world of appearances known to us is the world of which we are conscious, the world we represent. Thus if our consciousness is construed not merely as determined, i.e. not as merely reflecting given reality, but also as both indeterminate and determinable, then it becomes possible to develop the theory that the human mind is creative and formative. Our representations will then be understood primarily as indeterminately given (viz. as a successive manifold of representations referring to three-dimensional externality) and secondarily as determinate representations, viz. of organised nature. Our determinate representations —composing our inner empirical sense—contain perceptible nature; our logical synthetic faculty operates spontaneously on the indeterminate multiplicity of our representations, i.e. on the inner sense, transcendentally understood. If it can be shown that the spontaneous organ inherent in us (pure apperception) can validly form inner sense, then we can

SYNOPSIS

maintain that the reality we perceive and know is generated by the mind itself.

Before Kant can carry out his experiment—we may say of it that it aims to explain how nature, operating in accordance with necessary laws, is 'created' by the human mind, or how determinate nature arises from indeterminate nature—he must first decide and clearly establish what is to be regarded as ultimately indeterminate, i.e. what is originally given with potential consciousness. Kant's concept of the indeterminate must be as narrow as possible so that the compass and influence of man's determining faculties should be as wide as possible. Only a few elements may be assumed to be given. Otherwise his theory would lack the conviction of truth which is inherent in simplicity.

The three elements assumed to be given are matter, space, time. Given matter is completely indeterminate, a mere manifold to which the senses react in many different ways. Taken by itself, given matter is indeterminable. Given space is a three-dimensional indeterminacy capable of being represented as an infinite three-dimensional magnitude. Given time is indeterminate multiplicity capable of being represented as an infinite succession.

Corresponding to the given elements is our receptivity, which includes sensation and intuition; i.e. our receptivity is of such a kind that its sensations necessarily occur in the form of successive representations referring to three-dimensional externality. But within the human consciousness, logical spontaneity is combined with receptivity. For logical spontaneity operates on our receptive mind, i.e. on an indeterminate succession of representations relating to space—irrespective of whether such representations are sensible or pure, i.e. irrespective of whether they are described as sensations or not. In this way arises, to anticipate the argument, the phenomenal picture of organised nature.

We are now in a position to describe Kant's intellectual experiment.

II

The supreme spontaneous organ inherent in consciousness is called by Kant pure or original apperception. Speaking generally, it operates by transforming a given manifold into unity.[1] Such a transformation is to be regarded as a process of synthesis, and its product as synthetic unity.

The act of pure apperception is a logical act.[2] For the mind can organise the indeterminate which confronts us only by imposing upon it the relation of a higher order representation implying a lower order representation.[3]

Now this relation, produced by the action of pure apperception, is manifested in four ways or must conform with four norms. These norms correspond precisely to the four (twelve) kinds of judgement—the expression of all conceptual relation.[4] They are the archetypal forms of every thing objective; they are called categories. However, the categories by themselves can be neither comprehended nor described, i.e. they cannot be objects of our knowledge.

Now, the organ active within us does not operate on a mere manifold of representations; it operates on a succession of representations, i.e. on indeterminately given time. As 'productive imagination'—as it is now called—it transforms a succession of representations, inner sense, into an enduring representation which unites within itself co-existent representations, i.e. it generates the representation of determinate time.[5] Synthetic unity, realised as determinate time, is no longer merely something thought: it is an intuitable and conceivable representation. As such, it is the graspable archetype of all objects knowable by us; indeed, all further formal determination is contained in it.

[1] § 23.
[2] § 19.
[3] 'Of the logical use of the understanding in general'.
[4] §§ 9 and 10.
[5] § 21 I.

Synthetically ordered time as the archetypal form of thought includes:

1. Unity composed of numerical unities (category of quantity).
2. Unity as something real (in so far, namely, as time is materially filled: category of quality).
3. (a) Substance composed of its inherences (substance is the enduring representation composed of co-existent representations: category of relation: substance).
   (b) Unity in the case of a succession of states (this signifies necessity of succession: category of relation: causality).
4. Unity as what is possible, existent or necessary—depending on whether time is understood as determinable, or as determinate nature, or as a means by which nature is necessarily determined (category of modality).[6]

The human understanding legislates for the whole of nature by means of the four or twelve archetypal forms of thought or categories manifested in time—though we cannot say why there is this number of categories and not more, nor why precisely these categories exist and not others.[7]

Nature, in the transcendental sense, is space and time. Space is admittedly given to us, but not as something merely thought nor as empty space; it is given to us as nature, i.e. as materially filled.

The universe given to us is indeterminate space. It is given to us as an infinite, three-dimensional unity containing an infinite number of possible three-dimensional unities.[8]

Time is given to us as materially filled; it is given as nature.

The universe given to our consciousness is indeterminate time. It is given to us, namely, as an indeterminate succession of representations referring to (materially filled) space.[9]

[6] § 10.   [7] § 21.   [8] § 2.   [9] §§ 4 and 6.

Our spontaneous organ, operating on such a succession, generates the representation of the intuitable and conceivable entity in space. This representation, validly constructing by synthesis what is indeterminately given, contains what we call the object.[10]

But how do the categories make geometrical knowledge possible? How do they also determine the physical world perceived by us in all its sensible fullness?

Geometrical knowledge is knowledge of determinate space. But space is given as indeterminate space. Our spontaneous organ, which transforms a given succession of representations referring to externality into a necessary succession of unities in accordance with the category of quantity, first realises logical relations in space and makes them evident as divisible and measurable geometrical figures. In doing this it subjects the whole of nature to the laws of geometry. For space—primary matter, so to speak—forms the sensible or secondary matter contained within it in accordance with the form it itself receives.[11]

Finally, the mind, understood as empirical apprehension, is able to produce the natural object in all its fullness. For, affected by various sensations (successive representations), the mind, by categorically synthesising the given manifold, constructs the perceptible object in space and time. This object is objectively determinable, not only geometrically but also conceptually and through judgement. Similarly, the mind is able to generate phenomena which remain the same through various changing states. It does this by transforming given succession into something enduring, whose states are necessarily successive to each other.[12]

What has been said so far may be briefly, and in basic terms, summarised as follows.

My spontaneous organ of logical apperception generates the representation of organised nature by synthetically ordering my own consciousness. I shall remain unconscious of the given succession of spatial representations as long as that

[10] § 17.   [11] § 3; Kant's 'Introduction' V.   [12] § 26.

succession is merely indeterminate. Only by transforming it into a unified representation—i.e. only by converting it into a *single* consciousness—can I generate a determinate representation of objective nature.[13] Through the same action I also establish the representation of my phenomenal Self as an enduring subject confronting the successive representations of objective nature.[14]

The fact that I am capable of self-consciousness—indeed, the fact that self-consciousness must be able to accompany all my objective representations of nature—is to be regarded as proof of the critical theory. The reason is this: the representations constituting my Self and those constituting nature are, in content, the same; it follows that my self-consciousness can be based only on the fact that I am always capable of becoming aware of nature, not only as confronting me but also as originating within me. That is to say: my self-consciousness is, in fact, consciousness of my own spontaneity reflected in objective nature.[15]

III

The three categories of relation, applied to nature and expressed as judgements, correspond to the three basic laws of nature: the conservation of substance, causality, and community. These three categories dominate the whole of our knowledge of nature.[16]

1. Substance is a succession of representations transformed into duration. Various different representational contents are states of substance or phases of duration. Whatever states it may assume, substance is always determined by a synthetic act of the understanding, which orders time; viz. substance can neither increase nor diminish. That is to say: total substance or nature as substance is the totality of all possible representations understood as a *single* comprehensive enduring time.[17]

2. A perceptible natural event coincides with two

[13] § 16. [14] § 24 II. [15] § 16. [16] A 182–A 218/B 224–B 265.
[17] Cf. also the commentary to Kant's 'Introduction' V, 2.

necessarily successive states of the same appearance. But the principle of necessary succession is the principle of causality. Now, since the universe is the same as the succession of representations referring to space, i.e. materially filled time, it follows that our spontaneous faculty determines the whole of nature in accordance with the category of causality by imposing the law of determinate succession on time.[18]

3. Finally, community or interaction of appearances perceived in a *single* period of time also depends on a principle of spontaneous synthesis. Our spontaneous organ subjects the whole of nature to the basic law of community by transforming the mere succession of representations into the representation of enduring spatial unity, the elements of which are necessarily co-existent.

IV

We have already explained how our knowledge originates: it is based on intuitive, perceptual and conceptual representations of synthetic unity. It emerged that the nature of all knowable things is logical relatedness or union realised in the materially filled forms of spatial and temporal intuition. We can now add that this theory also circumscribes the sphere within which knowledge is at all possible, i.e. it clearly lays down the limits of all possible knowledge.[19]

It has become apparent that, no matter how far we take analysis, we shall never be able to know or even represent anything which does not have the properties of spatiality and temporality. It has, furthermore, become evident that all objects capable of being represented are synthetic unities and thus products of our own spontaneity. But this implies that our understanding, though spontaneously creative, will always be dependent both on a given multiplicity and on the mediating forms of intuition.

Hence, we may think of an intuitive intellect which is

[18] Cf. also the commentary to § 26.
[19] 'Phenomena and Noumena'.

independent of everything given; we may think of something which is not spatio–temporal, which is absolute unity—a unity which is other than unified multiplicity.

But the thought both of an absolute unity and of a non-spatio–temporal unity is utterly beyond our powers of conception. For anything conceivable by us must be thought of as a whole consisting of distinguishable parts; but in an absolute unity all distinctions vanish. Only an intuitive understanding for which all the distinctions necessary to us are inessential: only an understanding of which we may suppose that it creates both itself and the universe by simply becoming conscious of itself—only such an understanding could conceive absolute unity, i.e. the thing-in-itself. For us absolute unity must remain for ever unknowable.

A clear distinction between the phenomena knowable to us and the unknown thing-in-itself is thus shown to be indispensable. It should be further remembered that certain antinomies, i.e. problems apparently demanding a solution, are in fact the product of confusing phenomena and the thing-in-itself.[20]

The human mind, dissatisfied with the knowledge it is able to acquire, forms the representations of the total content of knowledge possible for us; as reason it postulates (1) finite unity and (2) a first immaterial cause of all material occurrences. But the understanding, limited to appearances, is incapable of transforming either of these representations into a concept.

1. Thus, to the question whether the world is finite or infinite there can be no answer. The world knowable by us is nothing other than our manifold spatio–temporal representations. Reason postulates finite unity or a totality as the final product of our many acts of representation. But our understanding, whose possible acts are infinite in number, is incapable of recognising any finite unity resulting from these acts, and it must therefore assume that the universe is infinite.

[20] A 405–A 567/B 432–B 595.

The critical explanation of this antinomy is as follows: the concept of absolute unity or real totality is beyond the powers of the human intellect, which is limited to synthetic unity and which can thus only represent ideal totality. The concept of absolute unity belongs to the thing-in-itself. If we were able to know the thing-in-itself, i.e. if the world were a thing-in-itself for our intellect, we should necessarily be able to know its real finitude or infinity, as the case may be. But the two representations of ideal finitude and ideal infinity are equally applicable to the phenomenal world.

2. (*a*) Man himself is a spatio–temporal phenomenon, subject to the law of causality. And yet he is also capable of acting according to the moral law, independently of material determination. Thus, although man is subject to necessary law, reason postulates that he is free.

(*b*) Reason postulates an absolute source or prime cause of the world; by this means it can be represented as finite. But the understanding, limited to knowable nature, demands that the totality of our representation should include that first cause, i.e. that the first cause should be partially or totally identical with the world. Hence, if the world is taken to be a thing-in-itself, it is incomprehensible that such a cause could be distinct from it; but if the world is taken to be *merely* an appearance, the possibility of a beginning not belonging to the appearance, i.e. the possibility of a first cause, is totally inconceivable.

The critical conclusion from this antinomy is as follows. The notion of creativity or absolute spontaneity is beyond our powers of comprehension. But if we distinguish between the phenomenon and the thing-in-itself we can reconcile both the representations of freedom and necessity, of the first cause and the phenomenal world. For this distinction is ultimately the distinction between independent-creative being and derivative created phenomenal reality. It is this distinction which alone makes it possible to think (1) of human nature both as spontaneous and legislative, and as sensible and determined; and (2) of the whole of reality both as divine and spontaneous, and as necessary and materially determined.

Our intellect, in the theoretical field, is, as we have shown, limited to appearance. It cannot penetrate to true Being; nor, as a result, can it decide whether there is an Absolute, a thing-in-itself, or not. But practical reason goes further than this. The moral law is inherent in us; human freedom consists in acting in accordance with the moral law and not under the necessity of sensibility. As a result, we may with complete assurance say—in spite of the fact that we do not know how this is possible—that we are free; therefore there is an ultimate creative power independent of the only world we know: the phenomenal world.

INDEX OF PERSONS

Aebi, 103
Adickes, 3, 83
Aristotle, 64, 65, 91, 114, 150

Berkeley, 59, 69

Collingwood, 6
Comte, 1

Descartes, 69, 138, 139, 181

Ewing, 203, 209

Fichte, 146
Fischer, 2

Hegel, 1, 117, 142

Hume, 3, 16, 17, 25, 31, 124, 127, 161, 162, 176, 193, 198, 203

Jaeger, 66

Kemp Smith, 3, 48, 49, 50, 52, 62, 68, 70, 71, 83, 85, 90, 94, 102, 104, 113, 116, 175

Leibniz, 3, 15, 44, 56, 58, 59, 60, 61, 176

Locke, 47, 122, 127, 180, 185

Maimon, 142
Mendelssohn, 2, 59

Newton, 3, 44, 56, 57, 58, 122

Paton, 3, 62, 75, 91, 96, 203
Plato, 65
Price, 47

Raphael, 47
Rosenkranz, 133
Ross, 65
Rousseau, 73

Scholz, 103
Schopenhauer, 1, 2, 133, 205
Siegmund, 103
Spinoza, 211

Vaihinger, 3, 62, 70, 71, 133, 168, 193
Vleeschauwer, 193

Windelband, 205, 210
Wolf, 44, 58, 59, 60

ANALYTICAL SUBJECT INDEX

analysis: presupposes synthesis, 109
analytic: transcendental, 88; distinguished from dialectic, 86
antinomies: product of confusing phenomena and noumena, 223; examples of, 223-4
appearance: definition of, 60-1; ordinary meaning of, 61; distinguished from illusion, 68-9; Kant's concept of, involves reality and objectivity, 69
apperception: pure or original, defined, 143-4, 218; principle of necessary unity of, 144-5, 149, 154; generates synthetic unity and organises the manifold, 90, 134, 138, 171, 176, 182, 191, 216, 218; Leibnizian concept of, 143
apprehension: empirical, 220; faculty of perceiving natural unities, 190; generates determinate space, 194; synthesis of, 190
a priori: logical and metaphysical distinguished, 15 (see 'judgement' and 'knowledge')
arithmetic, 24
association: of representations, accident and subjective, 156
attention: act of, 184
axioms: mathematical, analicity of, 27

categories: account of, 100, 106-7, 129, 132, 168, 170, 175, 190, 192, 201, 203, 218; applicability of: ideally to any kind of intuition, but actually only to ours, 154, 155, 166, 172, 174, 175, 178, 202; not applicable to thing-in-itself, 175, 188, 210; applied, 190; Aristotelian, Kant's criticisms of, 114; definability of, 111, 115, 132, 213; deduced from forms of judgement, 111; derived from a single principle, 93, 114; determine our experience, 190, 201; relation to judgement, 127, 129; of themselves yield no knowledge, 172, 201, 206; modal, 114; necessity of, 122; primacy of, 116; qualitative, 113-14; quantitative, 114; relational, 114; table of, 113; trichotomy of, defended, 117; ultimacy of, 116
canon: defined, 88
causality: 23-4, 104; category of, 196, 222; explanation of the validity of the category of, 193; and effect, 198; first, 223-4; and human freedom, 224; Hume's theory of, 197-8; Kant's theory of, 196-200; necessity of, 124
clarity: and confusion, distinction between purely logical, 60
community, 104, 116-17, 222

227

concept, 37; a priori, requires transcendental deduction, 121; a priori, includes categories and predicables, 127; as act of coherent thought, 94; empirical, 22; and judgement, 95, 97; pure concepts of the understanding, 89; traditional and Kantian theories of, 92; as synthetic unity, 92

conception: faculty of, 125; and intuition, 81; pure and empirical, 80; spontaneity of, 96

connection: product of human understanding, 147

consciousness: and apperception, 143; empirical, 158, 170–1; medium of intuition and conception, 126–7; objective, 157, 160; spontaneity of representation of own, 142; unitary principle of, 139, 144; unity of subjective, 157 (see also 'self-consciousness')

consistency: of critical philosophy, 1–3, 133, 206, 214

contradiction: law of, 28

Critique of Practical Reason, 202

deduction: empirical, 121; metaphysical and transcendental, 40; metaphysical, purpose of, 85, 121; transcendental, outline of argument of, 132–3; transcendental, comparison of first and second editions of, 133–4; difficulty of, 122; necessity of, 122; purpose of, 85, 121

dialectic: distinguished from analytic, 86; Hegelian, and its debt to Kant, 118; transcendental, 88

duration, 46–7

effect: see 'cause'

error, 70–1; Kant's theory of, 155–6; defined as non-valid or subjective construction, 155 (see 'illusion' and 'judgement, false')

experience, 14; objects of, generated by the categories, 126; defined as knowledge based on matter (sensation), 202

form, 9, 38; matter and, 209; Aristotle's theory of matter and, 64; not applicable to thing-in-itself, 209; Platonic forms, 65; universal and general distinguished, 65

freedom: human: definition of, 225; and law of causality, 224

geometry, 24; Euclidean, supposed to be only possible geometry, 171

God, 18; independent of space and time, 63, 71–2; transcends form and matter, 150

harmony: theory of pre-established, rejected by Kant, 125

imagination, 109; connective: can only produce subjective representations, 110; empirical, 194; cannot establish knowledge, 111; productive, 177, 179–80, 194, 218

ANALYTICAL SUBJECT INDEX

induction: cannot produce universally valid, necessary knowledge, 161
inherence: see 'substance'
intellect: divine, 150, 155, 170, 173, 206, 208, 209, 223; intuitive, 186–7, 233 (see also 'intuition, intellectual')
intuition: and conception, 81; empirical, 38, 80; form of, 38, 193; as form, 193; formal, 193; in general, 105; intellectual, 72, 97, 150, 174; viewed as a manifold which is unity, 142; outer and inner, 37; object of, 125–6; pure, 38, 80; sensible, but non-spatio-temporal, 72, 154, 158; not need the functions of thought, 123
is: as linguistic symbol of objective unification, 164

judgement: critical account of, 93, 103–5, 163; act of, 106–7; affirmative and infinite, 104; analytic, 19, 21; a posteriori, 19, 21; and category, 127; and concept, 93–8, 107; forms of, 112; as logical function, 168; as mediate knowledge of an object, 197; singular and general, 103; synthetic a priori, 19–20, 22–4, 30–1, 74; table of, 99, 101–2; traditional account of: criticised by Kant, 163; true and false, 70–1

knowledge: a priori, 13, 14–16, 83–4; a posteriori, 13; definition of, 87, 151; empirical, 161, 164–5; limits of, 18, 172, 222; mixed, 13, 16; objective, 164; practical, 211; problem of, 124; theoretical, 211; transcendental, 83–4; as union of intuition and conception, 78–80, 202

logic: applied, 81; constructive, 18, 94; foundation of intuition and conception, 166; pure general, a canon, not an organon, 88; Kant's reform of, 20–2, 76, 90–5; traditional, clarificatory function of, 76; traditional, comparison of, with transcendental, 21, 83, 90–1; Kant's re-interpretation of traditional, 91; traditional: relation to Kant's logic, 95, 100; transcendental, content of, 82, 100, 107; transcendental, definition of, 18, 81–2, 86, 111; valid for any created intellect, 174

manifold: connected, 135; empirical, 193; pure, must be assumed as given, 111; of intuition in general, 105; transformed into synthetic unity by conceptual synthesis, 109–10; unformed, 135
mathematics: axioms of, 24–5; analicity of axioms of, 26–7; not a form of transcendental knowledge, 173; synthetic a priori character of, 24–7
matter, 9, 38; Aristotle's theory of, 64; conservation of quantity of, 28–9; and form, 209; primary and secondary, 38, 74; and form, inapplicable to thing-in-itself, 209 (see also 'form')
memory, 109

metaphysics: impossibility of, 31; traditional and critical compared, 29-30
mind: as apperception, 189; as apprehension, 189; creative, 216; in what sense creative, 134-5; formative, 216; generates phenomenal nature, 141; productive, 79; as productive imagination, 179; receptive, 79; as faculty of conceptual spontaneity, 76, 140; as understanding, 179
modality, 101-2, 130, three moments of, 105
morality: connection of, with religion, 212; law of, exists as divine element in human nature, 211; law of, inherent in man, 225
motion: as determination of pure space by pure time, 52
movement: in sense of an action of the productive imagination, 183; two possible descriptions of, 52

nature: objectively determinable, 158; determinate and indeterminate, 170, 209; human: both spontaneous and legislative, and sensible and determined, 224; laws of, applied categories, 190; particular laws of, 201; generated by the mind, in what sense, 77, 81, 141, 188; phenomenal not noumenal, 141; as logically determined space-time, 64, 219
noumenon: negative: a limiting concept, 206; positive, 150; positive: object of divine intellect, 72; positive: not an object of knowledge for us, 206; positive and negative distinguished, 63, 205, 210; and phenomena, 205-13; as true object, 212

object: as appearances, but not illusions, 68-9; Berkleyan view of, as illusions, 68-9; definitions of, 77, 79, 151, 153, 176; in general, 17; in itself, 62; senses of, two opposed, 62-3; transcendent, 62-3, 212; transcendental, 212; true, noumenon, 212
organon: definition of, 88 (see also 'reason, pure')

paradox: element of, detectable in almost all of Kant's terms, 73
phenomenon, 38 (see 'noumenon')
predicables: product of logical analysis, 109; defined as pure derivative concepts of the understanding, 115
psychology: transcendental, 203-4

quality, 101, 129-30
quantity, 101; category of, explanation of the validity of, 193-4

realism: naive, Kant not guilty of, 69
reality: phenomenal, as the content of human consciousness, 138
reason, pure: canon of, 35; critique of, 33, 35-6; definition of, 33-4, 105; organon of, 34; system of, 33-5; and understanding, 32
receptivity: includes sensation and intuition, 217
relation, 101; three categories of, 221

ANALYTICAL SUBJECT INDEX

religion: and morality, connection of, proved ultimate and necessary, 212

representation: creative, sense in which, 126; defined, 79; faculty of, contains faculties of sensation, intuition and conception, 125; faculty of, object forming, 124; intuitional and conceptual, 151; construed as of an object, or as part of the self, 140; spatial, synthetic character of, 183

self: as content of thought, 139; as mere form, 150; generated by apperception, 184-5; intuitable by inner sense, 184-5; knowledge of, requires medium, 186; and non-self, basis of distinction between, 146-7; phenomenal, 59, 67-8, 181, 183-6, 221; unity of, 54; as thinking subject, 139

self-consciousness: conceptual faculty of, 170; consciousness of categorical synthesis, 131, 150, 171; consciousness of organised nature, 145, 221; consciousness of own spontaneity, 131, 221; creates self and nature, 138, 146; fact of, proof of critical theory, 140, 221; not involve absolute reality of self as Descartes had maintained, 181-2; transcendentally generated, 145; transcendental unity of, defined, 144

sensation, 37

sense, inner: form of, is time, 185; describable both as faculty and as its own object, 185; Locke's theory of, 185; not a spontaneous organ, 177; as receptive, 180; and the self as appearance, 180, 184-5; ordered by the understanding, 182

sensibility: defined, 80; and the understanding, 36

simultaneity, 48

space: absolutist view of, 57; critical view of, 40; empirical reality of, 45; given, 71-2; given, not to but with consciousness, 152; homogeneity of, 41-2; transcendental ideality of, 45; infinity of, 42, 75; intuition, 191; intuition and concept of, 43; as medium, 106, 108; presupposes that Euclidean geometry the only geometry possible, 171; as infinite given quantity, 75; realist view of, 40; relational view of, 40, 57-8; unity of, 41-2, 152; validity only for objects of intuition, 45; not valid for things-in-themselves, 44-5

spontaneity: definition of, 80; empirical or secondary, effect of the reproductive imagination, 159; logical, combined with receptivity, 217; primary, 'creates' objects in general, 158

subjectivism: transcendental, 203-4

substance: category of, 128, 221; conservation of, 221; Hume on, 161-2; Kant's theory of, 161-2, 195-6; Leibniz on, 176

succession, 46, 47-8

synthesis, 108-9; concept of, depends on possibility of synthetic unity, 135; conceptual, 110; figurative, 177, 179; intellectual, 177, 179; of the manifold, 177, 191; pure, 105-6, 110; activity of the understanding, 105, 136, 216 (see also 'unity, synthetic') *thing-in-itself:* determinate in itself, 61; identified with transcendental object, 62, 210; indeterminate for us, 59, 175, 208; knowledge of, impossible, 61, 208, 223; Leibniz's theory of, 59-60; limiting concept, 206; logical significance of, 209; metaphysical significance of, 209-10; object of divine thought, 210; relevance to philosophy of religion and moral philosophy, 211

thought: clarificatory, constructive and verificatory, distinguished, 91; coherent, definition of, 96; coherent, two senses of, 28; validly constructive, 110; formative, 135; intuitive, 150; and reality, 125; rules of, 99; spontaneity of, 136

time, 8, 24, 37; axioms of, 48; not a discursive concept, 49; determinate and indeterminate distinguished, 46-7; empirical reality of, 55; given, 71-2; given to us as materially filled, 219; indeterminately given, 135, 189; given as intuition, 191; given to but not with consciousness, 152; transcendental ideality of, 55; theory of ideality of, objection to, 56-7; Kemp Smith's objection to Kant's theory of, 50; laws of, 53; universal medium, 46-7, 50, 106, 108; possibility of mechanics, based on, 50-1; synthetically ordered, 219; realist view of, 57-8; relational view of, 57-8; unity of self, based on, 54

totality: category of, deduced from singular judgement, 113

truth: absolute, inaccessible to us, 139; Kant's concept of, 119; universal criterion of, 87; and knowledge, 87

understanding: activity of, is synthetic, 136; definition of, 105; as faculty of original and productive connection, 147; function of defined, 11, 96; legislates for nature, 190, 201; and reason, 32; transforms given manifold into a knowable object, 111-12; construed as absolute unity, 89

unity: absolute, 223, analytic and secondary, 112, 148; category of, deduced form general judgement, 113; definitional, 165-6; of Kant's thought, 4 (see also 'consistency'); logical, as object of interpretation, 4-8; non-spatio-temporal, 223; quantitative and qualitative, distinguished, 137; as synthesis of the manifold, 191; synthetic, 38-9, 165-6, 215-16; synthetic, objective, logical and categorical, 140; synthetic, possibility of, 135; synthetic, principle of, 91-2; produced by transcendental apperception, 134

universality: easier to understand than necessity, 16-17

will: moral, free from bondage of matter, 215